It is true in my life, the gateway to breakthrough has been through intentional prayer and fasting. Never have I sensed a greater need for seeking and knowing God. This book will give you steps to victory. Ronnie, this book helped me and challenged me!!!

—Dr. Johnny Hunt
President of the Southern Baptist Convention
Senior Pastor, First Baptist Church, Woodstock, Georgia

The Power of Prayer and Fasting is a much needed and timely book. Ronnie Floyd hasn't given us a book of theories. He has written out of his own life and experience. The stories are dramatic and powerful. These biblical principles are life changing. Ronnie practices what he preaches. He leads by example. He shows us the way to the Father, power, and revival. These truths have too long been on the back burner. Ronnie puts them at the forefront, where they belong. This book needs to be on your must-read list. If pastors and laity grasped the truths on these pages, we could see a great movement of God in our land.

—Michael Catt, Sr. Pastor, Sherwood Baptist Church in
Albany, Georgia
Executive Producer, Sherwood Pictures

In a day when so much of the church exhibits a form of godliness but will not submit to His power, Ronnie Floyd in *The Power of Prayer and Fasting*, opens the door for many to experience afresh the supernatural power of an awesome God.

—H. B. London Jr., Vice President
Ministry Outreach/Pastoral Ministries
Focus on the Family

Dr. Martyn Lloyd-Jones once asked, "In these days of exceptional evil, are you doing something exceptional?" In this new book, Ronnie Floyd will challenge and equip you to do something exceptional for the kingdom of God. I encourage you to accept the challenge!

—Dr. Steve Farrar, Men's Leadership Ministries

The Power of Prayer and Fasting reveals the true end of this neglected discipline: it is a gateway to intimacy with God; not an end in itself. It doesn't change circumstances or situations so much as it changes us. My dear friend Ronnie Floyd practices what he preaches . . . and that makes this book worth reading, and reading again.

—Ed Young, Pastor
Second Baptist Church of Houston, Texas

THE POWER OF PRAYER AND FASTING

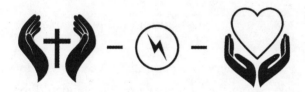

8 ESSENTIALS

TO EXPERIENCE SPIRITUAL BREAKTHROUGHS

RONNIE **FLOYD**

PUBLISHING GROUP

NASHVILLE, TENNESSEE

978-1-4336-9187-4

Published by B&H Publishing Group

Nashville, Tennessee

Mass Custom Edition

Unless otherwise stated, all Scripture quotations
are taken from the Holman Christian Standard Bible®
copyright © 1999, 2000, 2002, 2003 by Holman Bible Publishers.
Used by permission.

Also used: The New King James Version (NKJV),
copyright © 1979, 1980, 1982, Thomas Nelson, Inc., Publishers;
the New International Version (NIV), copyright © 1973, 1978,
1984 by International Bible Society; the New American Standard
Bible (NASB), © the Lockman Foundation, 1960, 1962, 1963, 1968,
1971, 1972, 1973, 1975, 1977, used by permission; and the
King James Version (KJV).

Dedication

To the fellowship of the First Baptist Church of Springdale and The Church at Pinnacle Hills, Arkansas, I dedicate this book. Throughout our twenty-three years together I have prayed and fasted for you, many of you have prayed and fasted for me, and we have prayed and fasted together many times. I am convinced that where we are today and where we are going in the future is to the glory of God alone. He has and is honoring all the praying and fasting that has taken place in and for this fellowship all of these years. To Jesus alone be the glory. Let's reach the world. Yes, all for Jesus!

A WORD OF CAUTION

Dr. Floyd is not a medical doctor. It is not the purpose of this book to advise you on the physical or medical aspects of fasting. *The Power of Prayer and Fasting, Revised and Expanded* is written from a spiritual perspective and is based essentially on the author's personal experience. There are some individuals, because of medical conditions, for whom a fast would not be safe. Anyone considering a fast should assess his or her own physical condition and consult a physician familiar with fasting before beginning.

Contents

Thank You

Jeana Floyd for being my friend and wife whom I love, as we have shared life and ministry together for thirty-three years.

Anita Stewart for helping coordinate some of this work for me with all the B&H team.

Tom Walters for believing in this work and wanting to see it revised and expanded for today's church.

B&H team, particularly Kim Stanford and Jeff Godby, for continually assisting Tom and me in this project. Your spirit and commitment to this work has been outstanding.

Andy Wilson and Ben Mayes for daily taking care of so many things in our church while I have had the opportunity to draw aside periodically to make contributions such as this around the world.

Foreword

This book is a major message of vast importance to God's people everywhere.

Dr. Ronnie Floyd combines his brilliant biblical insights and his profound experience with prayer and fasting to offer powerful, life-changing principles to every reader.

These principles can bring dynamic personal change, and they can bring national and world change, but these are not the most important potential effects. Far more importantly, these principles can help us to know our wonderful Lord better, more intimately, to draw nearer to Him, and to better experience His presence and power in our lives. And all these things, of course, help us to better glorify Him, to magnify Him with our lives, and to be more effective, fruitful vessels for Him to use.

Fasting with prayer is a spiritual atomic bomb in its potential power. Dr. Floyd shows you how to light the fuse. Prayerfully read, then prayerfully apply. You, and the world, will never be the same.

—Dr. Bill Bright (1921–2003)
Founder and President
Campus Crusade for Christ International

Preface

God can do more in a moment than I could ever do in a lifetime. I will never be the same for what God has done in my life and ministry through prayer and fasting. God used prayer and fasting to change me. His moving was significant, dramatic, sudden, and permanent. It penetrated the deepest level of warfare, providing breakthroughs to many obstacles in my life.

There is power in prayer and fasting. It is a means of access or entry into the supernatural power of God. Yes, it is God's gateway to spiritual breakthroughs.

As I write these words to you in the early morning of June 4, 2009, it was on this very day fourteen years earlier when God fell on our church with a genuine move of revival. On that Sunday morning in 1995, I stood in front of my church in deep repentance and brokenness, telling them about forty days that had changed my life. Coming off my first forty-day fast, God released me to share with them my journey, presenting to them what I believed was His message not only to me but also to our church.

God moved so significantly on that day. Even while I was preaching, people came to the altar weeping in deep repentance. What started at 9:30 a.m. that day did not end formally until after 12:00 noon. It blew up the entire morning schedule! The moving was so powerful, 70 percent of the morning attenders came back on Sunday night. Open confession and repentance of sin occurred, resulting in deep brokenness, powerful intercessory prayer, and a deep demonstration of worship and praise. The evening service that began at 6:00 p.m. did not end until 10:00 p.m. I will always remember it as the day *when revival came*. Revival is the manifested presence of God in our lives.

By no means would I ever believe my prayer and fasting made that day happen. It was a sovereign move of God. It was a great moving of grace. Yet prayer and fasting served as the impetus in my life that positioned me to encounter the manifested presence of God like never before. When God so radically moved in me, those around me were also moved by this breakthrough.

Imagine for a moment that God might manifest His presence in your life in a powerful, unusual, even supernatural way. Suppose He were to stand at your side, waiting to infuse your spirit with a fullness beyond your most cherished dreams or imagination. It would be a moment when God seems more real to you than at any time in your life. He would not be a God who for one moment cared about *business as usual*. Instead, He would invite you to join Him in the most exciting, provocative, creative adventure of your life, promising you that He was ready, willing, and able to carry you into an experience so lofty, so eternally memorable, that you would never be the same.

Would you accept His generous offer? If so, you would discover that He suddenly would no longer be the former familiar *God in a box*—perhaps the God of your childhood on whom you called to scare away bogeymen, or to help find the penny you lost in the grass, or the One you prayed would prevent you from getting what may have been a well-deserved spanking. But now, in your adult imagination, He has become infinitely more than your childlike perceptions. Suddenly you sense He is watching you with His keen eyes, ready to engulf you with arms of love and His all-embracing heart . . . waiting, waiting. You sense He is almost pleading for you to enter His streams of blessing through a designated gateway that He has chosen for you. What would prevent you from entering that gateway? Asked more positively, what would be some of the reasons you would *choose* to enter that gateway?

In the midst of the mundane and mediocre, consider the excitement of being moved by God through being touched by something out of the ordinary. Imagine how shattered and dull the routine of an average day would be in the presence of your creative, loving heavenly Father—a God who chooses to take you by the hand and lift you higher than you've ever been lifted before. All with His generous promise that you would be energized by hope that your most desperate, fearful, confused moments would dissolve and dissipate in His presence.

The good news is that what I've just described is not a dream. This fresh experience with your heavenly Father can be yours. That's because God is still God. He is still on the throne. He hasn't changed, nor will He ever change. The God of the Bible is the same God who is waiting and willing to work in the lives of people like you and me today. The God of the universe who spoke the world into existence, who knows the number of grains of sand on the seashore, and who also knows the number of hair follicles on your head, wants to unleash His power in you.

IN THIS CRITICAL MOMENT

I do not remember a time in my life when we needed God to unleash His power in us like we need right now. Fear is gripping our world like nothing I have ever seen before. Fear of a failed economy, loss of jobs, and threats of war everywhere has everyone on edge. In this critical moment in history, Christ followers cannot act like God is not trying to speak to us.

God is speaking to you and me. God is speaking to His church. God is speaking to America. God is speaking to the entire world.

We need to hear His voice and obey His call. I believe He is calling us to trust Him. Not ourselves, not our money, not our job, not even our country, but only Him.

Christ followers and churches cannot run scared like our God is dead. This is a time when we need to stand out and stand up like never before, declaring through our lives and with our words that our God is alive. He is still on the throne and in complete charge of everything. Our God reigns and we must live like He does.

The condition of my own life, my church, and America created a restlessness and desperation calling me into my first forty-day prayer and fasting journey. While matters were critical then in the church of America and in our nation, they are so much more critical today. Promise after promise from world leaders about a better future are given to us.

Yet, I know, in the deepest part of my soul, that *this time*, it is only God who is approaching us with a message which we can embrace completely. He comes toward us with His compelling vision for a better future.

When we are ready for His fresh, loving touch, God appears. He moves us off dead center. Our small lives and shallow perspectives are challenged as we stand in awe of His holiness. The white heat of His holy presence penetrates our lives, and we are transformed. Once again God works in ways that are out of the ordinary, defying natural explanation. His love is above and beyond anything we can think, imagine, or expect. His power is supernatural. It is beyond the natural, common, everyday experiences of our lives. The question is not, nor has it ever been, whether God is willing to move in the hearts of His people; the issue is whether we are willing to surrender in full obedience to Him so that we may begin to enjoy the enormous blessings He invites us to enjoy by living in His presence.

Now is the time for us to experience times of refreshing that come only from the Lord. If your schedule is over-whelming you, or your stuff in life is distracting you from the presence of God, it is time to stop and pursue God again. The alarm clock is going off in your life, in the church, and in our nation. This is not the time to push the snooze button.

It is time to wake up. It is time to answer the call. God is ready to provide you with powerful spiritual breakthroughs that will change your life, filling you with hope like never before. *Do not ever forget these words: God can do more in a moment than you can do in a lifetime.*

His entry point and means of access to this is prayer and fasting. Yes, prayer and fasting are not only powerful, but they are God's gateway to spiritual breakthroughs. We need breakthroughs in our lives. We need breakthroughs in our churches. We need breakthroughs in our country. We need breakthroughs in our world. It is time we stop drinking the Kool-Aid of false messages that will eventually end in utter hopelessness.

Desperate times call for desperate actions. This book is calling you to higher ground than perhaps you have ever been before. Awaiting you is God's power. As we approach Him humbly, we will begin to live in radical obedience to Him. We will learn God is not our buddy, but He is God, Holy God, and we will be in awe of Him. When we see Him as He really is, our response will be absolute surrender, being emboldened about the future like never before. As these matters begin to be experienced personally, we will arise together in the church to pursue God in the same way we have done personally, and that is in prayer and fasting. Ultimately, while all of this is occurring, we will begin to see the church experience God like never before in our generation.

Are you ready? God's gateway to supernatural power and spiritual breakthroughs is prayer and fasting. Consider it. At some level sometime in your life, whether it is only a lunchtime, or a day, or three, seven, ten, or even forty days, could God be calling you to pursue Him in prayer and fasting?

God's power is before you. You can *know* the power of God. Let's talk about it. Better yet, let's experience it together. I cannot wait. Come on. Go with me now.

For nothing will be impossible with God.
—Luke 1:37

He told them, "This kind can come out by nothing but prayer and fasting."
—Mark 9:29

Chapter One

Knowing the Power of God

We operate computers so powerful that we can be in touch with the entire world. The world is flat due to this powerful tool called technology. We energize our bodies with power breakfasts and consummate important business deals over power lunches. We wear clothing at times that projects a power look, depending on our power taste. Powerful modes of transportation exist on land, through the air, and on the sea. We read books that give us the 1, 2, 3s of achieving unlimited power. Self-help CDs and DVDs guarantee us all the power we'll ever need to be successful in business and in our personal lives.

Power, power, power. But for all the promises made, and the vast number of good intentions laid out before us, someone invariably comes along and yanks on the plug, turns out our lights, and leaves us in darkness once again, forcing us to fend for ourselves as we go back to square one, defeated, out of gas, and powerless. Why do we do this to ourselves when the power of all power is only a prayer away?

Jesus proclaimed the power of His Father in some remarkable ways. One expression of His power was through *signs and wonders*. The laws of nature were temporarily put on hold as Jesus fed a mountainside of people with only five loaves of bread and two fish. A leper was made whole, to the surprise of everyone. Men of faith made a way and lowered their disabled friend through a roof so Jesus could touch him and heal him. Lazarus was raised from the dead, an event to be followed later by the ultimate in death-defying feats—the resurrection of God's only Son. All of these were awesome and, you would think, convincing expressions of God's power.

In challenging the early church to embrace God's power, Paul often spoke about preaching that is effective—not because of its human wisdom but because it is energized by the power of the Spirit of God. The core message of the New Testament is that the power of God changes lives, transforms points of view, moves nations, and makes people new creatures. Power is a recurring theme throughout the Scriptures, but still, for many of us, we have only begun to understand the full ramifications of this power in our daily lives.

While we continue on our frantic search for the next promise of power, personal fulfillment, and self-gratification, God stands at our side, patiently waiting and holding a connection that will give us one of the greatest sources of power we will ever know. It's a source of power still unknown, underused, misunderstood, and even fear evoking in the minds of some people. Pure and simple, it is the power of God that manifests itself through prayer and fasting.

This power is so great that regardless of the obstacle, breakthrough is possible. It can become a thrust that penetrates the deepest darkness of spiritual warfare. Its advance can be so militant that it can break through the highest, thickest, and deepest wall that may exist before you. When the power of prayer and fasting is discovered and developed in your life, you will experience spiritual breakthroughs that Satan had convinced you were impossible to occur. Ah, the entry point into knowing this kind of supernatural power of God is prayer and fasting.

Let Me Tell You My Story

Although the discipline of prayer is frequently taught and practiced among Christians, the experience of knowing the power of God that comes through fasting, at least until recent days, seldom has been addressed in our generation. Even though fasting and prayer have been part of my life since my collegiate years, they have definitely taken on a new dimension in the past two decades of my life.

I have been active in the church most of my life and have attended too many religious meetings and conferences over the years to count, but until the mid-1990s, I cannot recall a single occasion when a call to fasting was given center stage. I don't remember ever receiving any instruction on fasting or what it could do for my spiritual walk. What little I did know, I picked up in my own study of God's Word. Early in my Christian experience, I made the decision to accept the Scriptures as the authoritative Word of God. As a result, what the Bible commands or teaches, I was determined to obey, even when I didn't understand its truth fully. Through this commitment to biblical truth, I began to catch a glimpse of the power of God that could and would become manifested in my life through fasting and prayer.

I was a freshman in college when I first became fascinated with the many references to fasting in the Bible. I discovered and defined it: *fasting is the abstinence from food with a spiritual goal in mind. It is when I pursue the God of Heaven to do something powerful and supernatural in and through my life.* This is what I interpreted through the study of God's Word; therefore, I was ready to believe and practice it. Immediately I began to practice fasting in college for one-, two-, or three-day fasts. They were integral to my walk with God. All of this prepared me for the life adventure God had before me.

Fast-forward to Monday, January 15, 1990. My wife, Jeana, was diagnosed with cancer. I couldn't believe the news. My young, beautiful wife—with cancer? How could this be? I was desperate and found myself truly powerless in dealing with the fear of not knowing what the future would hold. I knew I needed God's power at this difficult time in our family's life, and so I began fasting one day a week that entire year, asking God to heal my wife. On a fasting day, in the early morning in prayer, God gave me a word from Isaiah 43:1–3 about my wife. I believed He was promising to heal her.

Through God's anointing and blessing the work of doctors and nurses that performed surgeries, or conducted and monitored radiation and aggressive chemotherapy treatments, and by God's healing power, my wife is alive after all these years. I believe God placed within me great faith and wisdom from His Word through weekly encounters of prayer and fasting, all for the healing of my wife.

Her story and that entire story are so fascinating and such a testimony about the power of God. You can read more about it in her book, *An Uninvited Guest: One Woman's Journey from Cancer to Hope.* When you read it and share it with cancer victims and their families, both victims and family members will hear of God's amazing power. We believe this power is awaiting us through the gateway called prayer and fasting.

I'm not saying everyone should fast as I did, although I'm prepared to go on record as saying I know of nothing more powerful in my Christian experience. It has to be

God's call, not ours. Fasting must have a spiritual goal or purpose so important to us that we are willing to abstain from food, resulting in spending time with God for Him to speak to us. When we become so desperate for God that we have nowhere else to turn, we should enter into prayer and fasting. *Could our desperation be God's calling us unto Himself through prayer and fasting?* Let me set the record straight though: if God's command is to fast, then it's not an option. Jesus assumed we would as He said, *"When you fast."*

Through the next few years after my wife's healing, I began to fast and pray for one day a week for forty weeks a year. I would take matters to God that were deep on my heart. At times those "one-day journeys" might become three-day or more experiences.

In the winter of 1995, I felt God calling me to fast for forty continuous days. In the preface you read just a glimpse of that story. But friends, that story continues. What God did in me in 1995 was only the beginning of so much more. God has called me to at least five forty-day periods of fasting through the years. It is not something I counted or even remembered until I went to a closet with all my daily prayer journals that chronicle my spiritual life every day since 1990. There I discovered how many long-term fasts I have been on.

It has been *ALL for HIM.* I promise you, never had I desired to do any of those fasts until God put into my life the desire to do so. Each one of those long-term fasts has come from a divine calling created in moments of desperation to opportunities before me, or even obstacles I was facing at the time.

After that 1995 experience, God opened up for me to give the major convention sermon at the Southern Baptist Convention in the Superdome in New Orleans, Louisiana, in 1996. I will never forget right after I walked off the platform, Dr. Adrian Rogers, one of the leading pastors in the world at that time and who is now with the Lord, came to me, tears streaming down his face as hundreds of Christian leaders had responded to God's calling to repentance, humility, and revival during a public invitation to respond to God. He said: "I have prayed for and waited for this to happen in our convention all these years."

The story continued to unfold through a national event called *Stand in the Gap*. On a special October day in 1997, God drew 1.3 million men to the mall of Washington, DC, to pursue our God about our nation. I was given nine minutes to preach and was one of the few speakers who had been given that much time. God fell with great power upon that gathering and in those moments.

You see, preceding both of those significant and once-in-a-lifetime opportunities, it was in my daily time with God where He called me to be before Him for forty days of prayer and fasting to get His message for His people. So not only in 1995, but in 1996, then in 1997 again, for some reason, God called me to Himself in this manner. He was working in me in an unprecedented manner. Again, I share that humbly with you because it is just a small part of the story

God has created in me. By no means what God has done in me needs to become a principle for you.

At the same time, it is a biblical teaching that each one of us has to wrestle with at various points in life. Let me make this clear to you: I do not believe prayer and fasting are hoops we jump through to get God to do something in our lives. I do believe prayer and fasting get us into a position to listen and respond to God in a special way. Only by God's grace has any of this happened. This I do know: *every time God has called me to fast for whatever periods of time, He moves in my life profoundly.* I believe He will do the same for you.

Today I write these words freely to demonstrate that my response comes from biblical knowledge and conviction, followed by obedience to His Word, resulting in personal experiences I have had in deep moments of prayer and fasting.

As the sightless man whose only response to Jesus was, "Once I was blind, but now I see," so I, too, can say I have been changed inside and out. I am not the same man, the same pastor, the same husband, or the same father I once was. Fasting and prayer have been a gateway through which God has done supernatural things in my life, my family's life, and in my ministry. What God has done in me and in my church through fasting and prayer gave the church years ago a new pastor, and to me the pastor He gave a new church. And neither involved a change in our geography. This is a credit only to the power of God.

I am now also more convinced than ever that this miraculous gateway to God's supernatural intervention in the life of the believer is not exclusively reserved for a select few. It is the power of God available to everyone who trusts Jesus. It is the power of God for anyone who desires to enter the gateway called prayer and fasting.

LOST

If your days are like mine, then we both know we all need frequent touches of God's presence and power. No Christian I know of is immune from this need for a renewed experience with our heavenly Father. We may not always be mindful of His presence as we become distracted by other interests. Too often we are so thrown by the struggles of our lives that we blunt our focus, turn to other *solutions*, and throw aside our compasses—our only hope for a way out. We're lost in the deep woods of despair, wondering if we'll ever find our way home. You've been there, and so have I.

When we feel overpowered by our circumstances, intimidated by our challenges, and when we bleed over the pain of our wounds—an aching heart for relatives and friends who don't know Jesus, agony over illness that will not go away, worrying over job security, palms wet with sweat as we fear our economic future—or concern for the future of our nation, our need for God becomes obvious. When we have exhausted our energy, watched our most carefully laid plans crumble around us, and attempted every escape and remedy, the frailty of our fleshly existence meets us head-on.

Whether it's an individual, a church, or a nation, we are nothing apart from our Creator and our created purpose. When the reality of who we are and who He is sets in, that's the time to give up, cry out in desperation, lift our hands, and place our hope in the only One who can help us. Without this reliance on God's power, we will be doomed to live half lives, wallowing in mediocrity, never knowing the full joy of the Lord. Even as Christ followers, many times we feel lost.

The good news is that God is able to help us find our way and get our bearings in the journey of life. He simply waits for individuals, churches, and nations to acknowledge their dependence on Him and His grace. Only then will the spiritual power and blessings He has promised be showered on those who commit themselves to radical obedience and absolute trust. But this won't come easily. Spiritual breakthroughs are possible, but only by God's power. However, there will be a price to pay.

REVIVAL WILL COME

This gateway to God's supernatural power is prayer and fasting. The body of Christ must recognize these disciplines for what God has created them to be. They are the gateway to spiritual breakthroughs. Revival will come, the manifested presence of God will be experienced, when we pray and fast. When the church engages this age-old biblical principle, then the church will wake up and begin to stand up in our culture.

What is revival? It is the manifested presence of God in our lives. It is when we allow our heavenly Father to be free to live in and through us, move us, and shape us into the image of His Son. In my first forty-day fast, the Lord placed in my heart that He was going to bring a mighty spiritual revival to America that will transcend all denominational, cultural, racial, and ethnic lines. While moments have occurred in selected churches or regions of the world, we must see this kind of movement of God in America in our generation. The need is huge.

One of the people I follow on Twitter is Thom Rainer. Thom, president of LifeWay Christian Resources, is a gifted research specialist and understands the American culture. He sent a tweet that pointed us to a blog he wrote on May 28, 2009, about the millenial generation. It was a powerful blog, and I sent it out as a retweet. Now if you are lost with my jargon, it is just Twitter language. Let me talk to you about Thom's discussion in the context of revival.

Without revival we will lose much of our culture, but more sadly we will lose the next generation called the millenial generation. This generation was born from 1978 to 2000 and is the largest generation of people in the history of our nation. This group of 103 million people will become 40 percent of the eligible voters in the 2020 presidential election. By 2010 thirty-one million of these millenials will enter the workforce. This generation satisfies their social networking via text messaging, Facebook, and Twitter. Listen to this, my friend: *This generation is presently the most lost generation in our history as only one out of ten millenials knows*

Jesus Christ personally. While I love this generation for their dare and courage, as well as their enthusiasm and intellectual power, without a major spiritual revival, this generation will perish. Rainer tells us that they are the most open generation ever to the message of the gospel of Jesus Christ.

Just think—this is just one segment of our population. What about the rest of us?

We must call upon our God and His power so we can see this urgent revival occur. True spiritual revival will transcend anything we have ever experienced. It will change the way we think about ourselves, our God, our present, and our future. It will alter the behavior of our neighbors and friends. True revival will come when God is taken seriously by those of us who call ourselves *Christ followers*—take God seriously and finally believe what we say we believe. True revival will be akin to spiritual seismic activity, shaking us to our core, allowing us to see the profound overtake the profane, with the promise that our lives will never be the same.

This is why we must pursue the God of heaven in prayer and fasting. This is why at times we need to neglect food, or something else we love, spend that time with God in prayer and His Word, letting His power renew and refresh us so that the church can be revived. *I know this: without God's power we do not have a hope. But through prayer and fasting, we can begin to know the power of God like never before.*

It happened before. It can—and will—happen again. This spiritual revival and awakening will break the mold of all preconceived notions. It will rekindle the spirits and ignite the hearts of God's people. It will be exciting and dynamic. It will defy all human explanation. It will not be the exclusive product of any speaker or preacher, nor will it be owned or controlled by any denomination, self-appointed group of believers, spiritual group, or theological network. International borders will mean nothing.

When it comes, we will know it because it will be authentic and will spread like a raging fire in all directions. It could be as simple as a growing awareness of God's grace in our lives or as dramatic as a nationwide—worldwide—awakening. This true revival will result in countless thousands, perhaps millions, of people saying yes to Jesus Christ. It will mobilize the church ultimately to a Great Commission resurgence. We will have an insatiable passion to see every people group in our region, our country, and across the world won to faith in Jesus Christ.

I really believe revival will come before the Lord's appearing. I am more than hopeful; I am expectant.

WE DO NOT KNOW WHAT TO DO NOW

Second Chronicles 20:12 says, "Our God, will You not judge them? For we are powerless before this vast multitude that comes to fight against us. *We do not know what to do*, but we look to You" (author emphasis). With enemy forces breathing down their necks, the people of Judah were in the thick of trouble. It looked as if it was going to be total devastation for God's anointed. Even Jehoshaphat, the warrior king, was afraid. He became so fearful that he turned all his attention toward seeking the Lord in his life as he began to pursue God more intently than he'd ever done before.

In his terror at the prospect of massive defeat, the prophet proclaimed a fast throughout all of Judah. He asked the people to stop eating until God prevailed in their situation. He understood the spiritual practices of fasting and praying. Jehoshaphat knew that to fast before God was the best way to show his complete helplessness and humility before God. He learned something you and I must never forget: he renounced the natural to invoke the supernatural.

He declared, "God, I don't want food; I want You. You are more important than food." This was not a popular theme then any more than it is a driving principle in the hearts of large numbers of believers today. But it *is* a principle. It's a *revival* principle, a *resurrection* principle; and a resurrection always is most credible in a graveyard, an apt word for much of what we see in today's world. The self-gratification, self-worship, self-exaltation, and pagan moral principles that have infiltrated the church and encroached on our lives does not ask us to call on God for His strength and power. Not by a long shot.

The world keeps telling us to be more positive about who we are: "Live up to your potential. You can do it! See the glass as half full, not half empty. If it is to be, it's up to me! Every day and in every way things are getting better and better." Really? I hadn't noticed. This kind of thinking can derail us when we allow misguided counsel to subvert the Spirit of the living God. We really *do* believe that whoever ends up with the most toys wins. We want our cakes, our pies, our cars, our bank accounts, our stocks and bonds, our toys, our recreation, our steaks, and our mashed potatoes with gobs of gravy more than we are willing to feast on the bountiful riches and promises found in the Word of God. But when we're desperate, *we cannot have it both ways.*

Whatever stands in the way or is idolized in our lives has to go and take its rightful place. The truth is this: We are powerless in and of ourselves. And because physical food is not our ultimate source of nourishment, then physical food must be seen in its physical perspective: We, like the prophet, must be willing to renounce the natural to invoke the supernatural. Because of what God did through Jehoshaphat and others, we know what to do now. Why?

Jehoshaphat proclaimed a fast for his people so *they could once again see the face* of God. He said that they sought Him and kept their eyes on Him. When they became desperate, they shifted their focus to God and away from their hopeless, degenerate, discouraging, depraved situation. It was their choice, and it's also ours. When we become desperate enough, we, too, will drop to our knees, seek the Father, and keep our eyes fixed on Him, with the knowledge that one of the gateways to His supernatural intervention in our lives is through fasting and prayer; and this gateway opened the way for their spiritual breakthrough. God gave them their God-sized victory. No one could have done this but God!

When we are delivered from our despair by removing our focus from food to spending time with God, something takes place in our hearts that we can't control. Our spirits bear witness with the Spirit of God. Suddenly we say, "It's happened. God has finally stepped into my life. I've been delivered. I'm free. I've tapped into God's power in a supernatural way." Then something else amazing happens. Rather than getting on the phone to talk about the ball game or the latest rise or fall in stocks, we find ourselves saying, "Mary . . . Joe, I can't believe what God is doing in my life, and I just have to tell somebody."

God wants us to be conscious of His presence. He wants to give us hope for the present and confidence in our future. He wants to give us an attitude of thanksgiving that we've never had before. He wants to do something mighty in our lives, and that's why He provides us with moments of desperation—to push us toward Him. To better understand this principle, please read Michael Catt's *The Power of Desperation*.

Who is in charge of our desperate moments? God. Nothing happens to us that does not come first through His strong yet gentle hand. God is eternally up to something; we can count on it. When we become desperate, it will always be for a reason. It means God is speaking to us. He wants our undivided attention. He's demanding our uncomplicated allegiance. To have His way with His *always hungry* followers, He reminds us to pause often in His presence, remove the physical food from our table, and replace it with the bread that satisfies eternally, along with the nurturing water of the Spirit that promises us we will never thirst again. Now we know what to do.

ARE YOU DESPERATE TO KNOW GOD'S POWER AND EXPERIENCE SPIRITUAL REVIVAL?

I trust you are desperate, or else you would not be reading this book. This book is for those who really want, need, and desire a spiritual lift beyond anything men or methodology can do. There is a way, there is a gateway, and it is the gateway to God's power. That gateway is prayer and fasting.

Second Chronicles 7:14 says if, "My people who are called by My name humble themselves, pray and seek My face, and turn from their evil ways, then I will hear from heaven, forgive their sin, and heal their land." God wants to act on behalf of His people. But His actions are conditioned on the actions of His people. Humility in the presence of His power is what God demands of His children. Spiritual fasting is the *means*—the once-hidden, unexplored, misunderstood vehicle—by which we humble ourselves before God. If I knew another way, I would preach it from morning to night. But I know of no other way to be humbled in His presence. Only when we come to our heavenly Father in His way and on His terms and respond according to His agenda will He unleash His bounty of blessing and pour out His reservoir of supernatural power on our lives.

God's gateway to spiritual breakthrough is praying and fasting. The walls will be crushed, destroyed, and removed, and the power of God will fall. You can know the power of God via prayer and fasting.

Now is the time. Today is the day. If you are not desperate to see God move mightily in your life, confess it as sin, and then ask God to give you that kind of desperation. If you are desperate to see God move mightily, then take action now. Be willing to abstain from food with the spiritual goal of wanting to know God better, appealing to Him to unleash His power, and speak to you through His Word. He will supply your need for sustenance.

The truth is this: Life is not about food on the table. It is about being humble in the presence of God and being filled with the Bread of Life. That's the source of eternal satisfaction—the second secret in our discovery of God's gateway to supernatural power and breakthroughs.

 ## REFLECTION QUESTIONS

1.When is the last time you were desperate for God to move in your life or situation?

2. When is the last time you spent a day or a season in prayer and fasting?

3. Do you think that God may be calling you to a fast? If so, what is it you want to see God do?

Yet when they were sick, my clothing was sackcloth; I humbled myself with fasting, and my prayer was genuine.
—Psalm 35:13

He leads the humble in what is right and teaches them His way. All the LORD's ways show faithful love and truth to those who keep His covenant and decrees.
—Psalm 25:9–10

Chapter Two
Coming Humbly before God

Humility! We've all heard the story of the person who allegedly wrote the book *Humility, and How I Attained It* (now available in five volumes)! We laugh at this for good reason: Humility is tough. Unnatural. It goes against an insidious self-worship that's integral to our lives. We take pride in our looks, our accomplishments, the cars we drive, the money we make, and the houses we live in.

Unfortunately our lack of humility doesn't stop there. We brag about the most recent Bible study we attended or book we have read or debate over some theological issue. Matters like these and so many others result in airing our superiority and arrogance, looking down on others who may not be where we are. Hardly the thoughts of humility.

It reminds me of the English vicar who had six of his academic degrees painted on the glass door that led to his study. Underneath these symbols of decades of scholastic achievement were the words, "Your humble servant. Please make an appointment with my secretary."

While the Scriptures urge us on to perfection, they give us no encouragement to suppose that perfection will ever be achieved as long as we occupy this mortal flesh. Those of us who think for even a moment that we are righteous are not righteous at all. For this reason we are afflicted with a terminal disease called spiritual pride, the most deadly manifestation of our sinful nature. But what does it mean to be humble before God? Why is it important that we lower our estimate of ourselves in prayer and fasting before our relationships with God can move to a new level?

GOD'S WORD ON THE SUBJECT

Sometimes we may be reading the Bible too selectively and in the process we forget what God's Word has to say to us on the subject of being humble before Him. But when we take the time to search for God's truth in this matter, we read:

- But Gideon said to them, "I will not rule over you, and my son will not rule over you; the LORD will rule over you." (Judg. 8:23)

- This is what the LORD says: The wise must not boast in his wisdom; the mighty must not boast in his might; the rich must not boast in his riches. (Jer. 9:23)
- Then King David went in, sat in the LORD's presence, and said, "Who am I, Lord GOD, and what is my house that You have brought me this far?" (2 Sam. 7:18)
- The LORD is near the brokenhearted; He saves those crushed in spirit. (Ps. 34:18)
- He is able to humble those who walk in pride. (Dan. 4:37)
- Whoever exalts himself will be humbled, and whoever humbles himself will be exalted. (Matt. 23:12)
- Humble yourselves before the Lord, and He will exalt you. (James 4:10)
- Humble yourselves therefore under the mighty hand of God, so that He may exalt you in due time. (1 Pet. 5:6)

OUR MIDNIGHT CRISIS

Saint Augustine wrote, "Do you wish to be great? Then begin by being. Do you desire to construct a vast and lofty fabric? Think first about the foundations of humility. The higher your structure is to be, the deeper must be the foundation." It is no great accomplishment to be humble when the circumstances of life bring us to our knees. But to choose a humble spirit when we are praised is a rare occurrence and impossible in our own strength. This is why we have no alternative but to walk through the gateway to supernatural power with heads, hearts, and knees bowed low in humility before *God—the gateway of fasting and prayer.*

Because of the surrounding cacophony that screams, demands, and cajoles us to do our own thing, we need a clear, uninterrupted message from God to stay on course. The spiritual vital signs in this nation, in our churches, and in our individual lives display our desperate need for a word from God that hits us between the eyes, takes the wind out of our self-importance, reminds us that we are *not* God, and brings us to our knees. Why? Because we are living in a midnight crisis, and unless we humble ourselves with fasting and prayer, we will not know real joy, we will not know God's best for our lives, and we will never experience personal or national revival.

We need to stop long enough to evaluate where we are. Would anyone question that we live under ominous clouds of spiritual darkness? Unless we bow humbly before our God, that cloud will become even thicker, and the church will find itself increasingly immobilized, unable to support itself because of its own dead weight.

The answer to our spiritual crisis will not be found in the ballot box but in the prayer closet. The answer to our personal and corporate dilemmas will not come through high tech, hyperbole, and hype. It *will* come through a fresh touch from the Lord who wants to speak to us, move us, and manifest His mighty presence. Moving the furniture in our churches, denominations, or our own lives will not be enough. The answer to our spiritual crisis will come when we put off our mind-sets of self-worship, territorialism, and the spirit of arrogance and pride, and put on the sackcloth of prayer and fasting and humiliation and repentance before God.

THE POWER OF PRIDE

I am an expert on pride. When God brought major revival to my life, He addressed my pride dramatically. It was a Saturday night in the middle of a long-term fast. After wrestling in bed, not able to go to sleep, feeling as if God was calling me to prayer, I got up about 1:00 a.m. I was lying on the living room floor praying with my Bible open. God led me to Isaiah 57:15 that says, "I live in a high and holy place, and with the oppressed and lowly of spirit, to revive the spirit of the lowly and revive the heart of the oppressed." In that setting deep brokenness came upon me when I was indicted by the Holy Spirit for being a proud man.

I believe He said to me, "Ronnie, you are the problem in your church. You are filled with pride." There is more I could share here, but since being saved in high school I have always had a great passion to walk with the Lord, not able to remember a day since high school that I did not start my day with God. Yet it was on that floor God arrested me with His powerful presence. Since that moment I have never been the same.

Humility crushes the wall of pride in our lives. There is nothing more deadly than pride in our lives, and the only cure for pride is humility and brokenness. Humility destroys the wall of religious tradition. I have seen people fight for their religious tradition more than I have seen people fight for truth. We fight over matters that preserve our ways when in reality we are to be dead to all of them. This is not about us. It is all about Him.

Humility removes the wall of greed. Greed hoards the time, money, or possessions we have been entrusted with in life.

Greed exists because of pride. Why do people not honor God with the first tenth of all God has given them? Greed comes from pride. Humility is demonstrated through obedience to God's Word to giving; and when done, it removes the wall of greed. We can pray and fast for revival all day long, but we must stop the robbing from God that goes on weekly by the people of God. Many are stealing from God and still pastor churches, lead music, mentor adults and children, teach classes in our churches, and go on mission trips around the world. God help us get transparent before Him, getting honest that we are proud and full of greed. Only humility before God in giving removes the wall of greed.

Unforgiveness is prevalent in the lives of most Christians and in most churches. Unforgiveness occurs because of pride. I believe unforgiveness is the major obstacle to revival in today's church. Pride is so powerful that unforgiveness has become the norm in most Christ followers and churches. This pride has built such a calloused heart in us that we are no longer bothered by having an unforgiving spirit toward others.

Pride is powerful. It has destroyed men and women, families, businesses, churches, and governments. Most of all it has grieved the Holy Spirit in the lives of many of us. Has it done that in you?

Quite honestly, the only thing that will crush and remove the spirit of pride in us, is when we humble ourselves through fasting and prayer. When we humble ourselves before God with prayer and fasting, God will provide major spiritual breakthroughs. We will see breakthroughs regarding our pride, our religious tradition, our greed, and even our unforgiveness. God's gateway to spiritual breakthrough is prayer and fasting.

A Retro Crisis?

But what does the Bible say about this crisis? Has humanity ever been here before? Of course it has. Our crisis *is* a retro crisis. It's what the prophets themselves were most concerned about. It's the nature of our human condition when we go our own way, make our own rules, and put God on a shelf for a day *when we might need Him*. God's people in Judah were in a spiritual crisis continually. On one occasion drought and locusts served as God's judgment on their sin. The devastation was so great in the land that the people could not even offer grain offerings to the Lord. Their only hope was repentance. Enter the prophet Joel, who called the people of God to repent of their sin. That call is also for you and me to humble ourselves, pray, fast, and repent during this midnight hour in our world. Why? So, as we stand on this moment in history, we might experience a deep, life-changing moving of the Spirit of the living God in our lives.

Key spiritual principles in the book of Joel speak to our self-centered lives today. As our spiritual lives go, so go the spiritual lives of the leaders in our families, our churches, and our nation. Every one of us is a leader because we have influence over *someone*. We are either fathers, mothers, pastors, teachers, uncles, aunts, brothers, or sisters. In some area of your life, *you are a role model—a person of influence*. The question is: How well are you doing in your role? How is your influence being felt? Is it for good or for ill?

MODELING BROKENNESS

To enter God's gateway to supernatural power, you and I must model spiritual brokenness, humility, and repentance before the people of God and the world in which we live. Some things may be the worse for breaking, but a heart is never at its best until it is broken by the things that break the heart of God. Are we modeling this brokenness and repentance? Our answers will indicate the power of our spiritual lives. Hear the word of the Lord from Joel 1:9–20, a passage that speaks as confidently today as it did when God spoke it with power through His servant.

> Grain and drink offerings have been cut off from the house of the LORD; the priests, who are ministers of the LORD, mourn.
>
> The fields are destroyed; the land grieves; indeed, the grain is destroyed; the new wine is dried up; and the olive oil fails.
>
> Be ashamed, you farmers, wail, you vinedressers, over the wheat and the barley, because the harvest of the field has perished.
>
> The grapevine is dried up, and the fig tree is withered; the pomegranate, the date palm, and the apple—all the trees of the orchard—have withered. Indeed, human joy has dried up.
>
> Dress in sackcloth and lament, you priests; wail, you ministers of the altar. Come and spend the night in sackcloth, you ministers of my God, because grain and drink offerings are withheld from the house of your God.
>
> Announce a sacred fast; proclaim an assembly! Gather the elders and all the residents of the land at the house of the LORD your God, and cry out to the LORD.
>
> Woe because of that day! For the Day of the LORD is near and will come as devastation from the Almighty.
>
> Hasn't the food been cut off before our eyes, joy and gladness from the house of our God?

The seeds lie shriveled in their castings. The storehouses are in ruin, and the granaries are broken down, because the grain has withered away.

How the animals groan! The herds of cattle wander in confusion since they have no pasture. Even the flocks of sheep suffer punishment.

I call to You, LORD, for fire has consumed the pastures of the wilderness, and flames have devoured all the trees of the countryside.

Even the wild animals cry out to You, for the river beds are dried up, and fire has consumed
the pastures of the wilderness.

SPOT ON!

We are in the same condition as God's people during the time of the prophet Joel. This passage is spot on! The alarm is going off, and we must respond to it in America. It's time for the church of America to wake up, just as the priests and the ministers of the Lord in Joel's day were shaken out of their sleep over the sinfulness of Judah. If we are to know God's supernatural power, we, too, must have spirits that are contrite and broken. It broke the priests' hearts that they could not make any offering at all to God. God's judgment had been so mighty *that there was nothing left* to offer. They wept and wailed before the God of heaven. They humbled themselves through fasting. They demanded national repentance by calling for a solemn assembly to cry out to the Lord. Their tears were expressions of honest grief, and in their pain they interceded for the people of God. They knew this was God's gateway to spiritual power and His gateway to see spiritual breakthrough.

How broken are we today? In Jesus, *we* fulfill the role as a kingdom of priests.

How do you read this passage from Joel? Do you see it as another fascinating but perhaps ho-hum history of an ancient people who never seemed to be able to get it together spiritually? Or do you read these verses as a prophetic rendering of where you live today? If we take God's Word at face value, then these words from Joel *will* do something to challenge our hearts to take action.

They must touch us, break us, and drive us to a new desire to know God. When was the last time we were broken with grief over our own sins and alienation from our heavenly Father? When was the last time we confessed with tears that we were playing church games—just showing up so we could show off—while we knew we were little more than a sordid display of dead men's bones? When did we last intercede on behalf of our bosses, our colleagues at work, or the members of our own families with sorrowful hearts? When was the last time we fasted and prayed over our own spiritual plights, the spiritual conditions of our churches, and the spiritual health of our country? When was the last time we sensed God's calling us to repent of *anything*, especially our separation from the God who made us, loves us, and gave His Son for our eternal souls? When was the last time we were consciously willing to submit to His leadership and willfully to turn from sin when He called us to repent? When was the last time we called for a solemn assembly to cry out for God to forgive us and our brothers and sisters from our sins of racial prejudice, greed, lust, love of material things, and anything else that stands between us and God?

LEAD ON!

Have we ever been so humbled that we could hardly absorb the presence of God because we knew we were standing on holy ground? In our roles as leaders—and please remember, we *are all leaders*—have we ever been bold enough, tenacious enough, and spiritually concerned enough, to weep at the altar, asking God to bring a mighty spiritual awakening to our lives and to the lives of those around us? If we don't model spiritual humility born from our own deep experiences with God, if we don't model spiritual brokenness, and if we don't model repentance from our self-centeredness and demand for control, we will never see a spiritual revival in our own lives or in the life of our nation.

As we exercise our spiritual gifts and direct others to this gateway to supernatural power, we will be on our way to personal and national revival. God's people are the keys to this awakening in our time. It doesn't matter what the left-wing liberal does, and it doesn't matter what the right wing says. Denominations may have things to contribute—they'll always have things to contribute—however, our ultimate prayerful hope is that the church, the people of God, will address our own spiritual condition. This is not something any national or world leader can do for us. The church must rise up and lead on! *How do we do this?*

Joel 2:12–13 says:

> Even now—this is the Lord's declaration—turn to Me with all your heart, with fasting, weeping, and mourning. Tear your hearts, not just your clothes, and return to the LORD your God. For He is gracious and compassionate, slow to anger, rich in faithful love, and He relents from sending disaster.

Lead on in returning to God. Lead on in fasting and praying. Lead on in weeping and mourning over your sin. Lead on in brokenness. Lead on in returning to God through prayer and fasting.

Prayer and fasting are not optional. This is not about negotiating with God or trying to work out a "win-win" for the both of you, or acting as if everyone else is responsible. You are responsible. Your church is responsible. I am responsible. My church is responsible. Now is the time to lead on in America and the world God's way. God's way is with humility that comes through prayer and fasting.

When we do, this is what will happen. Read it slowly.

> After this I will pour out My Spirit on all humanity; then your sons and your daughters will prophesy, your old men will have dreams, and your young men will see visions. I will even pour out

My Spirit on the male and female slaves in those days. I will display wonders in the heavens and on the earth: blood, fire, and columns of smoke. The sun will be turned to darkness and the moon to blood before the great and awe-inspiring Day of the LORD comes. Then everyone who calls on the name of Yahweh will be saved, for there will be an escape for those on Mount Zion and in Jerusalem, as the LORD promised, among the survivors the LORD calls. (Joel 2:28–32)

If we lead God's way with prayer and fasting, *after this* God says, I will pour out My Spirit. Oh friends, God is waiting to give a mighty outpouring of His Spirit upon us and the church when we come before Him in prayer and fasting. Power and breakthroughs await all of us.

THE NEXT GREAT MOVE OF GOD

This will be the next great move of God! I want to be a part of it, don't you? God's gateway is prayer and fasting. Coming humbly before God is God's gateway to spiritual power and spiritual breakthroughs.

The stage is set in America. Desperation is at an all-time high in our generation. Most churches are missing demonstrations of major spiritual power. Most Christ followers are lacking the manifested presence of God in and through their lives.

God has our attention. A remnant of us must be desperate before Him. We must take action now to pray and fast. When we do, we will ascend the holy hill before God. *May God have mercy upon us and bring on the next great move of God.*

WILL YOU PAY THE PRICE?

I cry out to God for that next great move of God. As I fast and pray, God keeps telling me, "Ronnie, pay the price. Do what it takes. Get off your high horse of ego-centered living, and live for Me alone. Don't worry what anyone else says about you. You might feel you're all alone sometimes, but I'm with you. Stay with me in humility, fasting, and fervent prayer. Know that I am God and that I will heal your land. But I will not do it until you and others come to me humbly, with contrite spirits, and with your whole hearts. Your job is to tell my people what I've spoken for generations. If you are faithful in telling them what I said and if they truly love me, they'll do it. If they don't, they won't. You just keep on being my man. Revival will come to your heart and to your people."

I encourage everyone who fasts and prays—whether it is a one-day, two-day, weeklong, or extended fast—to keep a fasting journal. This record will become two things in your life: a *spiritual guide* to help take you where you want to go with God during your fast and an intensely *personal record* of what God is saying to you as you communicate intimately with Him *during* your fast. I consider my fasting journals to be pure gold, more valuable than any book in my library besides the Bible. They are filled with the words God has poured into my waiting heart. As I have reread my journals months later, I can see the issue of my human pride is one area where God continually worked with me. He was relentless. He would not let me go. He was the *hound of heaven*. And the more I saw my pride in contrast to His holiness, the more humbled I became in His presence.

OPENING MY HEART AND MY JOURNALS

I'm not very *public* with my journaling thoughts, but it seems more than appropriate to share certain passages with you. Here are some of my reflections, taken at random, from some of my forty-day fasts as I wrote them in my journal:

> God's purpose in my fasting is to humble me so I can give all my energies to Him, so He can enlarge my boundaries and use me in a greater way for His service. . . . I have had to go through the pain and endure the suffering to be used anywhere. God has given me a new power and authority.
>
> Lord, show me my pride as You see it in my life. Break me, God. Expose my sin to me. Empower me to repent of sin. Help me to seek Your face. Fill me with tears and a heart for personal revival, church revival, nationwide revival, and global revival.
>
> God, create within me an openness to You concerning all things, freeing me from any personal or

ministry bondage, so I can receive all that Jesus wants to give and demonstrate through me.

God, bring about a revival that will bring me humility, brokenness, the seeking of God, confession, and a repentance of sin that will fill me with tears and a heart for America and the world.

O Lord, show me my pride as You see it. I have been so blinded by it. Cleanse me of my pride. It is sin. It is a slap in the face of God. I believe I need You, God, to come over me with Your power and Your might. Unto you, Jesus, be the glory and power. I give it all up to You and Your power. I pray today would be the day when God falls on me. Empower my will. I pray for a God-happening. Lord, open my heart to Your Word. Thank You,

O God, for Your anointing. In Jesus' name.

Right now, God is wanting to usher in a great spiritual awakening across this land through this mighty gateway to His supernatural power, which provides the impetus for spiritual breakthroughs to occur. When it comes in power, this awakening will be the manifested presence of God in the lives of His people. It will cut through the clutter; it will demand we get our spiritual houses in order; and it will happen only when we keep our hearts and eyes focused on Jesus. This awakening will be nothing more or less than a fresh, new awareness of the importance of obedience to God. It will transcend all man-made barriers. It will come only when God's people humble themselves and pray, stand with God in His holy presence, and see sins for what they are: conscious, willful alienation from Almighty God. The immediacy of the hour calls us to act now—not later.

Revival will not come from the next election—as important as it is to exercise our right to vote. It will not come when the economy bounces back. It will not come because the car industry or the housing industry comes back strong. It will not come from playing church or maintaining the *status quo*. It will not come when we do not live like Jesus is Lord of every area of our lives. All of this is a guaranteed formula for failure.

Revival, and the spiritual future of our nation, will be determined by the people of God who will get down on their knees, pray, fast, and believe that God is bigger than their circumstances, bigger than any election, bigger than the Democrats, bigger than the Republicans, and much bigger than we are. While we are in a dark midnight crisis spiritually in our nation, through prayer and fasting spiritual breakthroughs await us.

WHAT WILL OUR KING JESUS SAY?

There was once a page in the king's court. He did not have many important responsibilities to carry forth until one day the king called him into the throne room. The king handed the boy a scroll, and on that parchment was written the following words: "In the prison across town there is a man who is going to be hanged today. I have decided to pardon him."

"Quickly," said the king, "take this message to the head jailer."

The little boy was excited about what he knew the king wanted him to do. He ran through the town thinking over and over about how grateful that prisoner would be, knowing he was now pardoned, and would not be hanged. As the boy passed a store, he saw some clothes and thought, *You know, the prisoner will surely need some new clothes for his new life.* So he went into the store and bought a splendid outfit for the one who would soon be free. He ran a little bit longer, and then, suddenly, he saw a place to eat, so he ran in and got some food for the convicted man because he knew the prisoner would be hungry. Then he started running with all of his strength toward the prison.

When he arrived, the young boy entered the jailer's office. With a smile on his face, the youngster took the scroll of pardon from the king and handed it to the head jailer. The boy said, "This is from the king himself. The man who was going to be hanged today is to be pardoned."

The jailer shook his head and began to cry. He said, "Oh, son, we executed that prisoner five minutes ago. He is dead. He is dead."

Tears welled up in the little boy's eyes as he walked out of the prison and headed back to the palace. As he shuffled toward the throne room, the guards could hear him mutter over and over and over again, "What is the king going to say?

What is the king going to say? What is the king going to say?"

Our King, the Lord of lords, Creator and Sustainer of all, King Jesus, is coming again. But before He appears, He wants to see a mighty awakening stirring in your life, in mine, and in the churches throughout this nation. If we don't choose to fulfill the spiritual challenges God has issued to us, we may one day walk away in grief, even as that little boy did. At that *kairotic* moment—our last, fleeting, propitious moment before the judgment, you and I will know in our hearts that God wanted us to do something great through His power, but that we, somehow, were too preoccupied with other distractions to meet the challenge.

Then, on our way to stand before our God, it will dawn on us just exactly what we missed. The breakthroughs were ours for the receiving, but we settled with where we were. As we approach the judgment seat of our Lord Jesus Christ, and come face-to-face with the King of kings, the fear of God will overcome us as we realize it is now too late in the day to humble ourselves before the Lord, too late to fast and pray, too late to help others see God's gateway to spiritual breakthroughs. As these thoughts slam into our hearts, we will find ourselves whispering those same words, *What is our King going to say? What is our King going to say? What is our King going to say?*

REFLECTION QUESTIONS

1. What are specific areas of pride in your life?

2. What are specific ares of pride in your church?

3. What do you plan to do about this pride? How are you going to humble yourself before God?

Holy, holy, holy is the LORD of Hosts; His glory fills the whole earth.
—Isaiah 6:3

Take your sandals off your feet, for the place where you are standing is holy ground.
—Exodus 3:5

But, as the One who called you is holy, you also are to be holy in all your conduct; for it is written, Be holy, because I am holy.
—1 Peter 1:15–16

Chapter Three

Standing in Awe of the Holiness of God

God honors everyone who stands in awe in His presence and serves Him with devotion and zeal. Jonathan Edwards, a faithful servant of God in colonial New England, was a shining example of a man with these godly qualities. Although his pulpit manner was not commanding, nor was he an extraordinary orator, many of his sermons had an overwhelming impact upon the people who heard him. What may be his most well-known message, "Sinners in the Hands of an Angry God," moved hundreds of his fellow country-men to repentance from sin, turning them to personal faith in Jesus Christ. According to some historians, that one address helped fuel the spark which became the flame that gave the eighteenth century a nationwide revival and out-pouring of God's power known as the Great Awakening.

This may indeed have been true. From a human stand-point, it will always be difficult to credit such far-reaching spiritual results to a single discourse. Still, there's no ques-tion God used His servant at a time in history when a no-holds-barred message was needed to turn hearts toward God. But if Edwards's single sermon was indeed a catalyst for this Great Awakening, it was not because of his personal charisma. This preacher's approach to speaking was calm—a surprise, perhaps, to some, given the fame of his singularly most famous sermon. His hands did not flail the air chasing the devil from his hell, nor did he gaze wild-eyed toward the sky, calling down fire and brimstone from heaven. His power was not human. It was God at work in the heart of a servant who had been to the Holy of Holies. What many have not realized is this preacher of revival had never been *more pre-pared* by God to deliver his Spirit-filled sermon.

GIVE ME NEW ENGLAND

Those who were acquainted with Jonathan Edwards knew that prior to the delivery of his message he had not eaten a mouthful of food for three days, nor, during that time, had he closed his eyes in sleep. Instead of pouring nutrients into his body, he sated his hungry soul with the food of the Spirit; instead of giving in to sleep, he pursued communion with His God that was as deep and far-reaching as any time ever in God's presence. Over and over Edwards was heard to pray, "O Lord, give me New England! Lord, give me New England!" Lathered in sweat and tears, when Jonathan Edwards rose from his knees and made his way into the pulpit that historic Sunday, those who saw him were transfixed, saying later that he looked as though he had been gazing straight into the face of God. Three days of fasting and praying had prepared his heart to preach the sermon of his life.

Edwards was praying and fasting for a spiritual breakthrough in New England. God responded to his heart and to his request.

Even before he began to speak, said eyewitnesses, spiritual dread and the heaviness of a conviction of sin fell upon his audience. And then he spoke his message, "Sinners in the Hands of an Angry God." He held his sermon notes so close that the audience could not see his face. He preached and preached until the people in that crowded assembly were moved almost beyond control. It's said that one man jumped up and rushed down the aisle crying, "Mr. Edwards, have mercy!" Others clutched the backs of the pews for fear of falling into the fiery pit of hell itself. Most thought Judgment Day had dawned. And for some undoubtedly it had.

Everyone in that assembly found himself standing in awe of the holiness of God.

Encountering the Holiness of God

Entering God's presence through prayer and fasting prepares the way for us to catch a glimpse of God's holiness. Adrian Rogers used to say:

> The church advances on its knees. Few things are talked about more in church than prayer, yet relatively few saints know and experience the marvels of intercession. The chief weapon against Satan is prayer. Satan has many strongholds, many bastions of strength in America today. To try to break them down with Madison Avenue techniques would be as worthless as trying to remove the Rock of Gibraltar by throwing snowballs at it. Satan sneers at our schemes, mocks our methods, laughs at our learning, but is paralyzed by our praying.[1]

This awareness of what our strength *is* and what it *is not* gives us our direction in the violent atmosphere of spiritual warfare in which we live. We cannot be salt and light and leaven to a world in despair by using tricks and methods that are at best ineffective. Questionable religious schemes always produce spurious results, the ecclesiastical equivalent of rearranging the chairs on the *Titanic*, hoping the singing of *Nearer My God to Thee* will somehow save the day. It never has and never will. To anesthetize the strongholds of the enemy is to come face-to-face with the holiness of God by entering His presence through fasting and praying with a repentant heart.

As we do, we learn that God has no need for us, but we have a desperate need for Him. His purity will be more than we can bear. His righteousness is so great that our feeble hearts will not be able to accommodate His glory. His sinlessness is so overwhelming that, in tears and with faces to the ground, we will be driven to see ourselves for who we really are—aliens from a holy God, distant from His uncompromising truth, suddenly discovering what we need most is to speak the words of the prophet Isaiah, admitting our own estrangement from our heavenly Father:

> Woe is me, for I am ruined, because I am a man of unclean lips and live among a people of unclean lips. (Isa. 6:5)

> Woe to those who are wise in their own eyes and clever in their own sight. (Isa. 5:21 NIV)

> "Woe to the obstinate children," declares the LORD, "to those who carry out plans that are not mine, forming an alliance, but not by my Spirit, heaping sin upon sin." (Isa. 30:1 NIV)

FROM FILLING TO EMPOWERMENT

During my times of fasting and prayer, God invariably directs my heart to verses such as these. As I read, I become broken in His presence, see my obstinate heart, recognize that I am of unclean lips, continually worshipping at the altar of self. Again and again I have had to admit before God that I still often try to hide my cleverness under a cloak of ministerial privilege. What I need now is what Jesus Himself experienced after He fasted and prayed for forty days while being tempted by Satan. He went up that desert mountain filled with the Spirit, but as Luke 4:14 reminds us, "Jesus returned to Galilee *in the power of the Spirit*, and news about him spread through the whole countryside" (NIV, author emphasis). It is essential that the Spirit of God fill us, even as it filled our Savior. But our strength for a life of witness comes when we, like Jesus, live *in the power of the Spirit*. If the gospel does not empower us to a personal awakening, if it does not make us sorrowful for a nation without God, and if we are not moved to want to touch a world that does not name the name of Jesus, we have failed to capture what it means to have been in the holy presence of God.

When working on the pages of my fasting journals, I felt the hand of God direct my pen as I wrote:

> Heavenly Father, break me, expose my sin to me, empower me to repent of my sin, help me to seek Your face. Fill me with tears and a heart for personal revival, church revival, nationwide revival, and global

revival. God, endow me with the authority and power of Jesus Christ in everything I do. Help me know Your holiness, whatever the cost. I am willing to pay the price for being in Your presence. God, pour out Your Spirit in such a way that a mighty revival and an awakening to Your power will break out among those who hear the message You have given me to share. God, give me a revival in my heart for those who don't know You, filling my mouth so much with Jesus that I will tell everyone I meet of my Savior and of His love for them, and how You can bring hope and healing to their shattered lives. Lord, I ask in Your mercy to create within me an openness to all things that are truly from You, holy God. Free me from any personal or ministry bondage so that I may receive all of You that You want to give me and demonstrate through me. God, show me Your holiness. Dear God, show me Your holiness.

God did not fail to show me His holiness. He also honored the desires of my heart and changed my spirit forever.

Each time I pray and fast for an extended period of time, I believe I have been moved to receive a special empowerment of the Holy Spirit. A special anointing is placed on me due to experiencing the God of heaven and the power of His holiness.

Inventory of the Heart

I have kept the following verses and their poignant, embarrassing questions close at hand during my fasts as a reminder that, if I was going to be serious about knowing God's holiness, I would need to look at an entire landscape of issues. I share these with you with a heart that invites you to be quietly honest with yourself and honest with God as you reflect on your answers. This is an important exercise, because when you and I choose to enter the gateway to God's supernatural power and live in the presence of His holiness, we must become persuaded that every yes to these questions suggests there is a sin for us to confess. I have long lived with these heart-piercing Scriptures and provocative questions.

Each time I have entered a period of fasting, I have always spent the first two or three days really living in and dealing with this inventory of the heart or one like it. I have found that God uses it greatly. Now get alone soon, take these questions, and walk before God having this inventory in your hand. Let it get in your heart. Ask God that His Holy Spirit would search you with His holiness and reveal to you any sin.

Now I share them with you and join you in this personal inventory of the heart.

1. *In everything give thanks; for this is the will of God in Christ Jesus for you.* (1 Thess. 5:18 NKJV)

   Do we worry about anything? Have we forgotten

to thank God for all things, the seemingly bad as well as the good? Do we neglect to give Him thanks for our breath, our health, and for life itself?

2. *Now to Him who is able to do exceedingly abundantly above all that we ask or think, according to the power that works in us.* (Eph. 3:20 NKJV)

    Do we shy away from attempting to do things in the name of our heavenly Father because we fear we are not talented enough? Do feelings of inferiority keep us from our desire to serve God? When we do accomplish something of merit, do we choose to give ourselves, rather than God, the glory?

3. *You shall receive power when the Holy Spirit has come upon you; and you shall be witnesses to Me in Jerusalem, and in all Judea and Samaria, and to the end of the earth.* (Acts 1:8 NKJV)

    Have we been hesitant to thank God for the miracles He has performed in our lives? Have we believed it's good enough to live our Christianity in a casual manner and that it's not all that important to share the good news of our deliverance with others? Are we sharing the gospel? Are we involved in advancing the message of Christ in our region, in America, and across the world?

4. *I say . . . to everyone who is among you, not to think of himself more highly than he ought to think.* (Rom. 12:3 NKJV)

    Are we overly proud of our accomplishments, our talents, our families? Do we have difficulty

putting the concerns of others first? Do we have a
rebellious spirit at the thought that God may want
to change us and rearrange our thinking? Do we
brag or boast to others about what we have? Do we
swell up with pride when we receive compliments?

5. *Let all bitterness, wrath, anger, clamor, and evil
speaking be put away from you, with all malice.* (Eph.
4:31 NKJV)

Do we complain, find fault, argue? Do we nurse
and delight in a critical spirit? Do we carry a grudge
against believers of another group, denomination, or
theological persuasion because they don't see the
truth as we see it? Do we speak unkindly about
people when
they are not present? Do we find that we're often
angry with ourselves? With others? With God?

Are we in harmony in *all* of our relationships?
Am I willing to let it go and start over again? Am I
right with everyone?

6. *Do you not know that your body is the temple
of the Holy Spirit who is in you, whom you
have from God, and you are not your own?*
(1 Cor. 6:19 NKJV)

Are we careless with our bodies? Do we defile
our bodies with unholy sexual acts? Do we overeat?
Do we take care of our bodies? Do we desire to be
fit physically?

7. *Let no corrupt word proceed out of your mouth.* (Eph.
4:29 NKJV)

Do we use language that fails to edify others, tell off-color jokes or stories that demean another person's race, habits, or culture? Do we condone these comments when guests are in our home or when our colleagues share them with us at work? Do we curse?

8. *Do not . . . give place to the devil.*
   (Eph. 4:26–27 NKJV)

   Do we close our eyes to the possibility that we may be a landing strip for Satan when we open our minds to him through ungodly practices, psychic predictions, occult literature, and violent, sex-driven, sexually perverted movies and DVDs? Do we seek counsel for daily living from horoscopes in the paper, on television, or on the Web rather than from God, our true and ultimate source for living? Do we let Satan use us to set up barriers that inhibit the cause of Christ in our churches and in our homes through criticism and gossip?

9. *Not slothful in business.* (Rom. 12:11 KJV)

   Are we chronically late in paying our debts, sometimes choosing not to pay them at all? Do we charge more on our credit cards than we can honestly afford to pay? Do we neglect to keep honest income tax records? Do we engage in shady business deals? Do we inflate our financial worth? Do we get in business partnerships with unbelievers?

10. *Beloved, . . . abstain from fleshly lusts which war against the soul.* (1 Pet. 2:11 NKJV)

Are we guilty of a lustful eye toward the opposite sex? Do we fill our minds with sexually oriented Internet sites, television programs, lewd movies, unsavory books and magazines? Their covers? Centerfolds? Especially when we sense no one is watching? Do we indulge in lustful activities that God's Word condemns, such as fornication, adultery, or perversion? Do we have relationships improperly on the Internet? Do we enter "chat rooms" we do not need to be in? Are we engaged in pornography in any way?

Are we practicing gambling or betting or playing the lottery in any way?

11. *Bearing with one another, and forgiving one another, if anyone has a complaint against another; even as Christ forgave you, so you also must do.* (Col. 3:13 NKJV)

Have we failed to forgive those who may have said or done something to hurt us? Have we written off certain people as not worthy of our friendship?

12. *Even so you also outwardly appear righteous to men, but inside you are full of hypocrisy and lawlessness.* (Matt. 23:28 NKJV)

Do we know in our hearts that we are often not what people see? Are we possibly hiding behind being active in our churches as a cover for our activities away from the body of Christ? Are we mimicking the Christian faith for social status, acceptance in our church or our community? Are we real?

13. *Finally, brethren, whatever things are true, whatever things are noble, whatever things are just, whatever things are pure, whatever things are lovely, whatever things are of good report, if there is any virtue and if there is anything praiseworthy— meditate on these things.*
(Phil. 4:8 NKJV)

Do we enjoy listening to conversation that hurts others? Do we pass it on? Do we believe rumors or partial truths, especially about an enemy or a competitor? Do we choose to spend little or no time each day allowing God to speak to us through His Word?

God is calling Christians to be authentic and transparent. Listen friends, you will be authentic in life if you are real before God. Genuine confession and repentance while in the holy presence of God will result in authenticity and transparency with everyone.

Changed Lives or Nothing at All

These are hard sayings and tough questions. At first, I hesitated to include these because they are so laser like, so straight to the heart, brutal, and to the point. Then the Spirit of God instructed me not to pull any punches. If we don't address these questions with honest hearts, the chances for personal renewal are virtually nil. We cannot play games with God and, at the same time, experience a spiritual awakening. Christianity in an unawakened America has already reached a level of diminishing returns. Richard Foster says, "People do not see anything to be converted to. They look around at these Christians telling them to agree to these little statements and say the enclosed prayer. They say, 'But you aren't any different from anybody else. So what am I supposed to be converted to?' We have to see changed lives."

Changed lives. *Results* from being in the holy presence of God. Changed attitudes, changed relationships, changed hearts. This is what can happen when we experience the supernatural power of God through fasting and prayer. When we repent of our willful desires to put distance between ourselves and God's holiness, He will change our attitudes toward our most cherished sins, and we will find ourselves in the center of a spiritual breakthrough. Only as we live in His presence will the power of the Holy Spirit enable us to change both our attitudes *and* our conduct. Instead of doing what our self-worshipping nature wants to do, we will choose to do what God wants us to do. When we experience God's holiness through fasting and prayer—giving up what is natural to attain a spiritual goal—we will never be the same. God will give us liberty. We will know the meaning of true worship. Our sinfulness, hopelessness, and insufficiency will come so clearly to the forefront that we, like the hearers of Jonathan Edwards's sermon—will know we are but one step from destruction. This is what can happen to us when we stand in awe of the holiness of God.

God Is Not Safe!

In the Chronicles of Narnia book *The Lion, the Witch, and the Wardrobe*, C. S. Lewis describes two girls, Susan and Lucy, getting ready to meet Aslan the lion, who represents Christ. Two talking animals, Mr. and Mrs. Beaver, prepare the children for the encounter.

> "Ooh," said Susan, "I thought he was a man. Is he quite safe? I shall feel rather nervous about meeting a lion."
>
> "That you will, dearie," said Mrs. Beaver. "And make no mistake, if there's anyone who can appear before Aslan without their knees knocking, they're either braver than most or else just silly."
>
> "Then, isn't he safe?" said Lucy.
>
> "Safe," said Mr. Beaver. "Don't you hear what Mrs. Beaver tells you? Who said anything about safe? Of course, he isn't safe, but he's good. He's the king, I tell you!"[2]

No Longer Strangers

The psalmist understood this awesome wonder when he wrote, "Taste and see that the LORD is good" and then urged God's saints to fear Him (Ps. 34:8–9). We need not cringe in terror, but we must live before Him with reverence and awe. Our holy God is not *safe*, but He is good. In fact, God is highly dangerous as long as we remain strangers from His grace. Our willful trespasses can no more exist in the presence of God than darkness can coexist with the light. To stand before God is to invite destruction, just as Moses knew he would have died had he looked into the face of God.

Then comes the comforting message of hope—that we are clean in our Father's sight, without spot or wrinkle, whole and healed. But this will not be a *cheap grace*. We are not allowed to take His holiness for granted. Nor are we to regard it as a theological concept to be studied and kept under lock and key. By definition, *holiness* means "to be separated and set apart," which is its purpose for us in our daily lives. Holiness will always have more to do with our inward lives than our outward expressions. Holiness will express itself with greatest integrity when our primary motive in life is the passionate desire to please God with our whole hearts. Holiness also leads to humanness—not depraved humanity, but life to be lived as God intended, perfectly expressed in the life of our Savior. America has perverted the concept of humanness. Rather than cherishing God's ideal for human life, we deify self and deny God. Only through Jesus Christ will we ever become truly human—the kind of people God designed us to be.

Without a regular encounter with God and His holiness, we will still default to a business-as-usual attitude toward God and life, just like the good ol' boy who came walking down the path from the Carolina mountains one day. He was all dressed up and carrying his Bible.

A friend saw him and asked, "Elias, what's happening? Where are you going all dressed up like that?"

Elias said, "I'm heading for New Orleans. I've been hearing that there's a lot of free-runnin' liquor and a lot of gamblin' and a whole lot of real-good naughty shows."

His friend looked him over and said, "But Elias, why are you carrying your Bible under your arm?"

Elias answered, "Well, if it's as good as they say it is, I might stay over until Sunday."

What Elias never learned was that when we spend time with God, we must change, even as we continue to function in the world of reality, touch real people, and make decisions about real problems.

Churches are full of people just like Elias. People attend, engage in worship, sing, serve, and yet have a sexual affair with another person while doing it. Or have some sexual relationship with Internet pornography or do not have business relationships that are wholesome.

We are in a day when so much of the world is in the church, it is hard to believe God even shows up on Sunday.

Yet, when we are with God, we will begin to have God's eyes and God's heart for people and situations. Not that we should ever shy away from the truth, but truth and compassion are both held in our hands.

This is where we are to live out the holiness God has given us, something that is neither outdated nor optional. Today endless programs of evangelizing stress everything but God's holiness. Most of our leaders are not valued for their holiness but for their ability to draw a crowd, thrill a crowd, and hold a crowd, thanks to their communication skills or political clout. How far this is from entering God's gateway to supernatural power. J. I. Packer says:

> Holiness is the very purpose of regeneration: that believers become Christlike. Nothing defeats Satan's purposes for Christians like a holy life, and nothing plays into his hands more than the failure to practice holiness. Holiness gives credibility to witness; lack of it negates the witness. True happiness comes only as a by-product of holiness.[3]

GENUINE WORSHIP

Worship is so talked about today. Questions and debates happen trying to discern what is and what is not worship. Interestingly, when Isaiah was in the presence of holy God, he understood his sinfulness. After he confessed and repented of his sinfulness, his life was changed dramatically.

He willingly offered to go and do whatever God wanted him to do.

Genuine worship is an encounter with God that results in lifestyle change. I hate to disappoint any of you, but it has nothing to do with the style of worship, or type of song sung, balance or imbalance, blended or not, casual or formal, tucked in shirt or untucked shirt, choir or praise team, or acoustics or band or orchestra. This is *us* majoring on stuff like these things thinking it will give us "an edge" or an appeal to more people.

Friends, genuine worship is biblical worship. Biblical worship is seen in Isaiah's life. He had an encounter with God, and he did not leave the same. Lifestyle change occurred. If we have not encountered God on Sunday or in our private worship, and we do not leave different than we came in or when we began, implementing something in life that makes us more holy, then we have not worshipped.

HOLINESS IN ACTION

A missionary in India was once teaching the Bible to a group of Hindu ladies. Halfway through the lesson, one of the women got up and walked out. A short time later she came back and listened more intently than ever.

At the close of the hour, the leader inquired, "Why did you leave the meeting? Weren't you interested?"

"Oh yes," the Hindu lady replied. "I was so impressed with what you had to say about Christ that I went out to ask your carriage driver whether you really lived the way you talked. When he said you did, I hurried back so I wouldn't miss out on anything."

So my questions to you and to me are these from an unknown poet:

> What would He find, should He come just now?
> A faded leaf or a fruitless bough;
> A servant sleeping, an idle plow;
> What would He find should He come just now?

What would He find should He come tonight,
Our garments soiled or a spotless white;
Our lamps all burning or with no light;
What would He find should He come tonight?

The privilege of living in the presence of God is open to every believer. Yet many of us settle for remaining outside that Holy of Holies, satisfied to grow weary and old in the outer courts of the tabernacle. What prevents us from entering this gateway where power and breakthroughs are occurring? It's not the character, nature, or actions of God, but the darkened veil of our own self-worship, a self-life that has not been carried to the foot of the cross.

When you pray and fast, your life becomes positioned to encounter holy God. When you encounter Him, the veils are lifted and the liberty begins. Breakthroughs occur because of God's power moving in your life. That is holiness in action.

HOLINESS LEADS TO INTIMACY

When we begin to experience the holy presence of God that comes through fasting and prayer, intimacy begins like nothing we have ever experienced before. Intimacy with God is a lifestyle. If it is to do its work, it must change us from within and cause us to review and alter our behavior in the heat and torment of our days.

Intimacy with God changed Moses on Mount Sinai when he prepared to give God's Commandments to His people. Intimacy becomes a reality when you and I say, "That's me, Lord," to the question posed by the singer of the psalm:

"Who may ascend the hill of the LORD? Who may stand in his holy place? He who has clean hands and a pure heart, who does not lift up his soul to an idol or swear by what is false. He will receive blessing from the LORD and vindication from God his Savior" (Ps. 24:3–5 NIV). Intimacy with the Creator means baring our hearts to the Father, allowing Him to see if there is any wickedness in us. And how quickly the verdict will be read. But it will be read in love, with encouragement, and a prodding for us to return to our families, our work, our schools, and our churches as different people because we've been in the presence of God.

Intimacy with God begins with long periods of quiet listening, only later to become a conversation where we ask Him, in His timing, to repair the terrible breaches in our relationships, to reveal our improper motives, to bring healing to our lives, to remove our spiteful spirits, to help us speak words of kindness, and to learn to express unutterable joy for the flash of flame that now blazes in our hearts for having been in His presence.

The fear of intimacy *(into-me-see)* with those significant people in our lives leaves us lonely islands of discontent— sometimes quiet islands, but often islands with angry volcanoes that erupt and spew their hate over the unprotected spirits of the ones we say we love. But when we've ascended the mountain of the Lord, lived in His presence, been cut to the quick by His Word, and have been drawn to His holiness in fasting and prayer, we need to fear intimacy no more: We will want to know others, and we will also want to be known. Earthly intimacy will have a direct correlation to our intimacy with God, a closeness based on trust, faith, and love in

Him. In our own strength, vulnerability and openness to others will remain a formidable challenge; but when built on an intimacy with God, we will be given the strength to take the necessary risks to make intimacy with those we love a growing part of our lives.

Do you see it? Prayer and fasting move us into moments of self-examination spiritually, resulting in encountering our holy God personally. When we begin to see lifestyle change occur in us due to this, we move to the kind of spiritual breakthroughs where intimacy with God occurs. Please know, standing in awe of the holiness of God will lead to an intimacy with God so special that your passion becomes *living in obedience to God*.

 ## REFLECTION QUESTIONS

1. Can you recall a special moment when you were in the presence of God where His holiness was sensed greatly?

2. What are the personal sins in your life that need to be dealt with in repentance?

3. Does the worship in your life and church lead to lifestyle change?

They grumbled in their tents and did not listen to the LORD's voice.
—Psalm 106:25

I will always keep Your law, forever and ever. I will walk freely in an open place because I seek Your precepts. I will speak of Your decrees before kings and not be ashamed.
—Psalm 119:44–46

Chapter Four
Living in Obedience to God

Sir Leonard Wood was once invited to visit the king of France. It was such a pleasant experience for the king that he invited his honored guest to return and immediately set a time for dinner at a later date. When the day finally arrived, Sir Leonard returned to the palace. The king, meeting him in one of the great halls, said, "Why, Sir Leonard, what a surprise. I did not expect to see you. How is it that you are here today?"

"Did not your majesty invite me to dine with you?" asked the astonished guest, fearing he may not have come at the appointed time.

"Yes, that is correct," replied the king, "but you didn't answer my invitation."

Sir Leonard answered, "But your majesty, a king's invitation doesn't need to be answered, it must simply be obeyed."

Obedience is not a natural phenomenon for most of us. As children, we struggled to obey, terrorizing our parents with the most perplexing and unnerving questions we could possibly ask, and asking them nonstop: "Why do I have to do that, Mommy?" "Why can't I do that, Daddy?" As students, it was not much better, since we usually felt we'd probably be a lot better off if the administration would allow us to make the rules. And as adults, I have a sense we've not made a whole lot of progress in the obedience department.

Like a Good Pilot

"A good pilot does what it takes to get his passengers home," writes Max Lucado. "I saw a good example of this while flying somewhere over Missouri. The flight attendant told us to take our seats because of impending turbulence. It was a rowdy flight, and the folks weren't quick to respond; so she warned us again. 'The flight is about to get bumpy. For your own safety; take your seats.'

"Most did, but a few didn't, so she changed her tone, 'Ladies and gentlemen, for your own good, take your seats.'

"I thought everyone was seated, but apparently I was wrong, for the next voice we heard was that of the pilot. 'This is Captain Brown,' he advised. 'People have gotten hurt by going to the bathroom instead of staying in their seats.

Let's be very clear about our responsibilities. My job is to get you through the storm. Your job is to do what I say. Now sit down and buckle up!'

"About that time the lavatory door opened, and a red-faced fellow with a sheepish grin exited and took his seat.

"Was the pilot wrong in what he did? Was the pilot being insensitive or unthoughtful? No, just the opposite. He would rather the man be safe and embarrassed than uninformed and hurt."[1]

This is why another pilot, Chesley "Sully" Sullenberger, the pilot of US Airways Flight 1549, is such a hero as he landed this flight safely on the Hudson River. His successful emergency landing on January 15, 2009, saved the lives of 150 passengers and four other crew members. He was a hero to America but in that critical moment he was just doing what he was trained to do.

Just as experienced pilots do what it takes to get their passengers home safely, so it is with God. He looks into the empty, cavernous depths of our hearts and knows our deepest thoughts, even when we are not always fully aware of our inner world, and He knows what we need to do. Our heavenly Father knows, in this world of high-decibel noise and permanent distraction, we will often fail to hear His voice. But He knows what we must do. When we think we need another class in self-improvement or a fresh prodding of our human potential, God simply asks us to obey His voice. When we're busy reviewing the blueprints to build our self-contained lives, hoping *this will* provide for our better future, God says, "Child, obey Me. I have better plans for you." When we think we finally have our lives under control because of our enormous wit and will, God tugs at our hearts, opens the pages of His Word, and asks us to read the gentle demands He's made on His children over the ages:

> He was diligent in every deed that he began in the service of God's temple, in the law and in the commandment, in order to seek his God, and he prospered. (2 Chron. 31:21)

> For just as through one man's disobedience the many were made sinners, so also through the one man's obedience the many will be made righteous. (Rom. 5:19)

> And this is love: that we walk according to His commands. This is the command as you have heard it from the beginning: you must walk in love. (2 John 6)

Seeing with New Eyes

Obedience to the commands of God comes through physical solitude, exterior silence, and by entering His holy presence through the spiritual disciplines of fasting and prayer. This is not an esoteric experience where we escape to a desert, climb a lonely hilltop, or retreat to the quietness of our family room for study without purpose. Our objective has never been more focused: *It is giving up physical food with a specific spiritual goal in mind.*

It would be presumptuous to attempt to guess where you find yourself in your spiritual journey. That is neither my purpose nor my desire. But I do want to try to persuade you to look at your life with new eyes—through the eyes of one who now may be starting to see that God has more for you than you ever imagined. To come to that conclusion, you must make your own decision that there's more to life than news, weather, sports, and ordinary religion. There must be more to your life than taking the kids to soccer practice, washing dishes, meeting deadlines, devouring fast food on your way to another meeting while on your cell phone booking another meeting, and ending up so drained that you wonder if you'll have the strength or the guts to make it through another day. And the harsh beat goes on until you're beaten to the ground. Whispering through the noise, Jesus is saying, "My child, there is a better way. Come into my presence. I will give you rest. Trust Me and obey."

Throughout history, those who have allowed God to give them a set of new eyes, received fresh vision in their lives. They have also testified to the necessity of fasting in their lives. John Wesley instructed his followers to fast twice each week and would not ordain a man to the Methodist ministry if he didn't do so. Others who recognized the importance of fasting as their spiritual worship and discipline include Martin Luther, John Calvin, John Knox, Matthew Henry, Charles Finney, Andrew Murray, and D. Martyn Lloyd-Jones.

When we are willing just to obey the biblical call to prayer and fasting, we will receive a fresh set of eyes. We will begin to see much more that God wants to do with us and through us.

THE FAST I HAVE CHOSEN

Solitude, quiet, and being set apart from the distractions of this world are vital to hearing God speak. If possible, I hope you'll be able to read the following verses in a place where you will not be disturbed or interrupted. If you feel so inclined, ask God to use this portion of Scripture from Isaiah to speak to your heart, to give your life new direction, and to demonstrate to you the kinds of results you, too, can expect when you live in obedience to God through fasting and prayer.

Is not this the kind of fasting I have chosen: to loose the chains of injustice and untie the cords of the yoke, to set the oppressed free and break every yoke? Is it not to share your food with the hungry and to provide the poor wanderer with shelter—when you see the naked, to clothe him, and not to turn away from your own flesh and blood? Then your light will break forth like the dawn, and your healing will quickly appear; then your righteousness will go before you, and the glory of the LORD will be your rear guard. Then you will call, and the LORD will answer; you will cry for help, and he will say: Here am I.

"If you do away with the yoke of oppression, with the pointing finger and malicious talk, and if you spend yourselves in behalf of the hungry and satisfy the needs of the oppressed, then your light will rise in the darkness, and your night will become like the noonday. The LORD will guide you always; he will satisfy your needs in a sun-scorched land and will strengthen your frame. You will be like a well-watered garden, like a spring whose waters never fail. Your people will rebuild the ancient ruins and will raise up the age-old foundations; you will be called Repairer of Broken Walls, Restorer of Streets with Dwellings.

If you keep your feet from breaking the Sabbath and from doing as you please on my holy day, if you call the Sabbath a delight and the LORD's holy day honorable, and if you honor it by not going your own way and not doing as you please or speaking idle words, then you will find your joy in the LORD, and I will cause you to ride on the heights of the land and to feast on the inheritance of your father Jacob." The mouth of the LORD has spoken. (Isa. 58:6–14 NIV)

These verses are filled with great truth for us. The results of our obedience are God sized.

WE CAN'T MAKE IT ON OUR OWN

Sometimes in life we need the help of another person—a stronger person, a wiser counselor, a friend who can provide us with a perspective we cannot gain from our most noble efforts. The good news is that we already have such a friend. Perhaps we are troubled with physical infirmities, the mental or emotional pain of a family that's falling apart, or a financial crisis that is looming and has us scared to death, leaving too much month after the money is gone. Whatever our circumstances, there are—or soon will be—times when we will either choose to travel the highway to God's spiritual breakthroughs or opt for the low road of confusion, conformity, and compromise. Isaiah has a word for us at this point in our restless, distracted, out-of-control, overbusy, overcommitted lives.

We must consider ourselves blessed that God, through His prophet Isaiah, has provided us with twenty-two promises (results) in these verses from Isaiah 58. We can expect to receive from engaging in the spiritual disciplines of fasting and prayer—inseparable twins designed by our heavenly Father to usher us quietly into His presence. I have seen each of these promises come true in my walk with God, and I'm confident they can also live in you, through you, and will be yours as you call on God to do His will in your life. I encourage you to read and reread the above passages and sort through the twenty-two results you can expect from your time with God in prayer and fasting. I share my thoughts on seven of these promises.

Promise 1: Freedom

When we pray and fast, God promises that He will liberate us. He will loose the chains of injustice. He declares that He'll untie the cords of the yoke and will give the oppressed their long-awaited freedom. He will set us free from the bondage of what others think, making us realize that any comparison we make with others is a guaranteed fast track to misery. When we fast and pray, God steps in and frees us from the perceived alienation with Him that has kept us immobilized, fearful, and disobedient for so long. Freedom means we don't have to go to God to keep confessing the same, tired old sins we've been confessing all our lives because God will give us power to do as we ought.

We are all too much like the faithful deacon who, week after week, would pray fervently, "Oh Lord, in Your mercy, I beg You to clean the spiderwebs out of my life."

A fellow deacon, after hearing this prayer for too many months, in desperation finally prayed a fervent prayer of his own: "Oh Lord, in Your mercy, kill the spider."

We need to move on in freedom. As we come humbly into the presence of God in fasting and prayer, we begin to see our bondage in stark relief. Our sins show up clearly. What we were confident was acceptable, personal goodness and righteousness turns out to be, as the Bible tells us, little more than filthy rags. But that's it exactly! It's that bold awareness of our alienated human condition that compels us to cry out for the liberation of our spirits. Before long, we learn there is a way of escape from our self-imposed prison.

As you consider God's call to fasting, perhaps for the first time, you may choose to start slowly, fasting and praying for only one day. Perhaps you'll decide to fast and pray one day each week throughout the year where you declare that specific twenty-four hours as your time of obedience to be alone in the intimate presence of God. I would suggest you begin your fast at 6:00 p.m., writing down the things for which you believe God wants you to fast, remembering that fasting is abstaining from food *with a spiritual goal in mind.* As you do, God will give you grace, comfort, and a new direction in your Christian walk. In the end you will be set free.

One of the great stories of freedom was shared with me by a man who was hooked on pornography for many years. He began to pray and fast, desiring freedom. God began to reveal to him all sorts of sins in his life, not just pornography or his involvement in homosexuality. The warfare during the long forty-day fast was intense. Battle after battle occurred. Finally, toward the end of the fast, God brought miraculous freedom to this man not only from other sins but also from his main demonic strongholds, pornography and homosexuality. From what appeared to be his course, set for life since childhood, God released him from miraculously. He testified that he believed with all his heart that prayer and fasting were God's gateway to his experience of super-natural power and spiritual breakthroughs.

Just as he was set free, you can be set free also. Regardless of your challenge or sin, God can give you a breakthrough!

Promise 2: Oppressed No More

When we fast and pray, God promises to break every yoke of oppression that crushes us. What's it like to be oppressed? We feel so ground down we wonder if we'll ever rise again. We've done our best, but it apparently wasn't good enough for some, and we became a bull's-eye for their mounting fears, anxieties, and hostility. The dictionary says that *oppression* is "the burdensome, unjust exercise of authority or power." It's precisely that.

Some studies suggest that 95 percent of us feel oppressed in one area or another of our lives. Why? Because in most cases we have chosen to be oppressed. We'd still rather remain in our bondage, calling for room service to come to the prison cells of our minds, rather than reach around and throw open the bolt to the unlocked door! God is the One who has opened that door for you and me. He's already picked the lock. When we choose to walk through that door in obedience to His will through fasting and prayer, we receive God's anointing and power. That's also when we finally see our own self-worship for what it really is, an unholy act of pretending we are God and we have the wherewithal to run our own lives.

But when we give up food for an established period of time, with a specific spiritual goal in mind, we realize we are standing in the holiness of God's presence. We begin to hear, perhaps for the first time, His generous promise that our yokes of fear and bondage will be broken, that we are no longer oppressed by other "authorities and powers," and that because He empowers us, we *will* be free. The oppression of our pasts will no longer afflict us. The oppression of a negative spirit that is destroying our lives and hurting others will be left at the foot of the cross. Our oppression from problems so staggering that we feel we will never find solutions will be history. This is the power, the supernatural power, we expect when we come in obedient faith to the feet of our Savior.

Too many Christ followers live life settling for where they are. Yet God is able to set them free from their oppression. All is possible through God's power, and many times that kind of power only comes when we pray and fast.

Promise 3: Learning to Share

When we fast and pray, God teaches us how to share with those who have physical and spiritual needs. "Is it not to share your food with the hungry and to provide the poor wanderer with shelter—when you see the naked, to clothe him, and not to turn away from your own flesh and blood?" (Isa. 58:7 NIV). The book of Proverbs complements this passage by reminding us that when we give to the poor, we lend to the Lord. It's hardly the slick approach to personal success and advancement. Instead of asking God to breathe His vitality into our lives, we have been sold a bill of goods on which most of us have already taken delivery. Instead of sharing with the truly needy, we become experts at piling up toys for ourselves. We somehow felt the more things we could accumulate, the greater would be the panacea for our ills—at least that's what the promotion promised.

But the package was full of Dead Sea thinking. Like the Dead Sea we take in without giving out. We take, take, and take some more with little thought of giving to others. We take in sermons for ourselves but seldom pass their lessons on to those who are confused about life, lost and dying without a Savior. We fill our homes with still more *things*, but we seem to keep these material blessings for the exclusive use of John and Mary and the kids, we four and no more. So much around us is Dead Sea thinking.

Our self-help books promise us fame and fortune but are seldom able to deliver. The bill of goods so much of radio and television programming sells us is hard to believe. Our self-congratulatory infomercials feature pitchmen who hit us up on late-night television with the promise of be-all-to-end-all skin cream that will not only make us look fantastic but can also help us finally say good-bye to those ugly little wrinkles forever. We're prodded to buy the latest, greatest exercise machine so we will have rippling abs and steel-strong thighs—as if that's the main reason God created us. We are promised we can make big bucks in real estate with no money down so we can join the ranks of those millionaires who allegedly now live on Easy Street because they saw the light and got in early on the deal.

Meanwhile the widow goes hungry. The child without a father gets caught up in a gang, and the die is cast for a life of misery and pain. Orphans continue to need homes, the hungry continue to need food, the down-and-out continue to need clothing, and the widow continues to need care. Where is the sharing of the abundance of our hearts? When will we begin to believe and act on what we say we believe?

Fasting and prayer put the self-life into perspective. These spiritual disciplines force us to ask ourselves: *Is this all there is? Is there not something more to live for than living for self?* When such a prayer reaches the heart of God, He will respond, "My child, if you would enjoy a life of true liberty, see My face in those who suffer. See the needs of struggling humanity here and abroad with My eyes, hear their cries with My ears, and you will be blessed. I will show you the way you should walk, but you must come to Me humbly, obediently, in prayer and fasting."

You are never more like God than when you give. Prayer and fasting can build within you the character to give. Giving is a joy, and we need to be willing to pour ourselves out to those who can do nothing for us in life. We need to be willing to pour out ourselves to anyone, anytime, anywhere. This is the heart of Jesus, and it needs to be our heart. Prayer and fasting build within you the power to give.

Promise 4: Our Light Shines

Through prayer and fasting God takes our dim, half-light of tentative faith and increases its candlepower so our lights can break forth as the dawn. We cannot look directly into the rising sun without damaging our eyes. Yet that's the kind of brilliance God promises will light up our lives and, in that glow, bring light to those dimmed spirits who continue to live in darkness. But it even gets better: "Then your light will rise in the darkness, and your night will become like the noonday" (Isa. 58:10 NIV). A noonday sun is even brighter than the sun at dawn—and God is still talking about us. He's making us a promise that this will happen to *our* lights when we come to Him in fasting and prayer. We are indebted to The Christophers for their insightful motto: "It is better to light one candle than to curse the darkness." For you and me, it may start with that one candle today, perhaps another candle tomorrow, until we see that God is illuminating our lives with a beam of light that shows us who we really are and why we need a Savior. The darker the day, the brighter our lights will become when we fast and pray.

As I observe those who have fasted and prayed over an extended period of time, I can always see that the lights from the spirits of their inner persons glow more brilliantly than ever before. That's because death to self is profound; then we experience an awakening to who we are in Jesus Christ. *This* is what brings a glow that God alone can give to people when they fast and pray. It's what brought such a radiance to the face of Moses when, on the mountain with God, he came face-to-face with his Creator. When we fast and pray, we, too, will begin to experience the glow of God that only comes when we go one-on-one with Him.

Just as the glow of God was on the face of Moses after his seasons of fasting and prayer, God's glory will shine through you. People will know you have been with God. Your countenance will reflect the glory of God.

Promise 5: Healing for Body, Soul, and Spirit

"And your healing will quickly appear" (Isa. 58:9 NIV). Healing. Becoming robust and healthy in body, soul, and spirit. This is what our world cries out for: "Please deliver me from the pain. I can't stand it any longer. Will there ever be relief for my hurting body and struggling soul?" That's why we buy more pills than any nation on earth, yet most of the sickness is in our thinking. We're told the majority of people in hospital beds have no clinical reason for being there. *And your healing will quickly appear.* Is the Bible a medical book? No, I don't believe it is. But it does offer a divine prescription for what ails us, and it declares its truth in the context of fasting and prayer.

Many of us are stuffing ourselves with too much of the wrong food, drinking too many diet drinks, and loading up on too much fat. We are ruining our bodies with cholesterol, caffeine, and chemicals, refusing to exercise, and ingesting so much unnecessary over-the-counter medications that our bodies don't have a chance to function as God intended. We have choked the life, power, and potential from what God has called our *temples.*

Fasting and prayer contain this healing element. I have seen the Lord heal various challenges I have had, but through prayer and fasting, healing has taken place. Since fasting has become integral to my spiritual worship, I have been delivered on many occasions.

Was it the fasting that gave me relief? Was it the elimination of poisons and toxins from my body that brought on my healing? I don't have any idea, and it doesn't really matter. I just know I feel like the blind man healed by Jesus who couldn't explain how it all happened but was robust in his testimony when he said, "I was blind, and now I can see!" (John 9:25). I believe God healed me. I have no reason to think otherwise. Our bodies, when given the opportunity to walk in obedience to God, *can* be cleaned up and healed to be the highly functional *temples* our heavenly Father designed them to be.

Promise 6: Protection from the Father

Have you ever observed a mother hen looking after her young? If she sees a hawk circling overhead, she instinctively gives a warning sound, and immediately the baby chicks come running to hide beneath her wings. When menacing storm clouds fill the sky with rolling thunder and jagged lightning, she quickly makes a noise that calls her brood to herself where they find protection from the elements. As night approaches and the shadows lengthen, she gives out yet another, quite different, call that gathers her young to rest.

When we come humbly into the presence of God in prayer and fasting, our Father promises us protection: "Then your righteousness will go before you, and the glory of the LORD will be your rear guard." Protection from the front and protection from the rear—God literally has us covered. And for good reason. Satan remains on the loose, roaming about like a roaring lion, seeking whom he may devour. As fasting and prayer become integral parts of our lives, we find ourselves over-whelmed by God's care for us, especially as our lives continue to be sprinkled with everything from daily annoyances to outright fear.

Fasting and prayer will keep the enemy at bay. They are our spiritual shields. If you find it somewhat difficult to agree with what I am saying, perhaps you have not yet put yourself in a position to experience God's supernatural power in your life—a power available to you right now. It's simply not possible to live in the presence of our Protector and not feel the touch of His gracious, comforting hand that keeps our souls at rest while the storms rage around us.

When we fast and pray, we can expect two things: (1) We will enter spiritual warfare as never before. That's why we must be prepared with spiritual weapons. We are taking over enemy territory. (2) We can know with all confidence that we are protected by God in the front and at the rear. Our encouragement comes from those who have walked before us in the confidence of their God—people like the apostle John who wrote, "Greater is He (the Lord Jesus Christ) who is in you than he who is in the world" (1 John 4:4 NASB, parenthesis added). Satan is our enemy, but God's protection is near at hand.

Promise 7: Answered Prayer

As you pray and fast, you will call on God, and He will answer you. Answered prayer is the quintessence of praying and fasting. If I were to share with you the five or six pages of the prayer journal I prepared prior to my first forty-day fast, and then walk you back through my journal since then, you would see one thing: *My prayers were answered.* There is something to the disciplines of prayer and fasting. I could point you to every experience of long-term fasting where God has answered my requests before Him. This does not mean they were answered as I preferred, but it did not matter. He had worked in my heart, and I was released, fully confident that God was ordering my way.

I only know that when Ronnie Floyd humbled himself enough to remove food as his focus to make the commitment to praying toward a spiritual goal, when he quit trying to run

80

his own life, when he finally gave up his best-laid plans and sincerest human efforts, and when he deliberately turned his life over to God once and for all, his prayers were answered. That's all I can say, "I was blind, and now I can see!" (John 9:25). My experience with God's answer to prayer then—and today, as I continue to fast and pray—has ushered me into a new spiritual environment where I am no longer surprised at *any* of God's blessings. If anything, I humbly *expect* my prayers to be answered by a generous, Almighty God.

When we humble ourselves before the Father, and when God sees we are serious about giving Him our broken spirits, He begins to do things we have never seen before. It's empowering. It moves us to another level in our Christian life. It sensitizes us to the needs of others at home and overseas as we suddenly find ourselves quietly praying for people, events, and situations with the knowledge that our prayers not only will be heard but that the Father will answer them.

Please understand: Prayer and fasting prepare my heart to receive whatever God wants to do in my life. As I present my request to Him earnestly, whatever He determines to do is easy to live with. Why? Because my heart wants what He wants, not what I want. Prayer and fasting position me to hear God speak and receive what God does.

INSUFFICIENT IN OUR OWN WISDOM

One evening Henry was in his pharmacy when a young girl came to get some medicine for her sick mother. He hurriedly mixed some drugs, put them in a bottle, and gave it to her. She took it and ran off as fast as she could. But as he was putting the various vials back in place, he was horrified to see that he had used one containing a strong poison. He didn't know the girl, or where she lived. Perhaps the mother was already taking the deadly prescription. A cold sweat broke out on his forehead. Then at his wits' end, he remembered a verse of Scripture that went something like, "Call on Me in a day of trouble; I will rescue you" (Ps. 50:15). He began praying for salvation as he asked God to help him.

Suddenly the young girl reentered the store in tears. "I ran so fast I fell and broke the bottle," she exclaimed in distress.

Greatly relieved, he gave her the correct medicine. That harrowing experience got Henry's attention, and it's reported that from that day forward he lived for Christ and became a different man.

Coincidence? Luck? Or God's timing and *answer to prayer?* Does fervent prayer make any difference? It did to Henry, the young girl, and her mother. And this experience can also be yours. Abraham Lincoln once wrote, "I have been driven many times to my knees by the overwhelming conviction that I had nowhere else to go. My own wisdom, and that of all about me seemed insufficient for the day." Only when you and I arrive at that crossroad and make the same decision as Mr. Lincoln will our hearts be ready to hear God's call to come to Him in humility and obedience.

- *Obedience:* Doing something because it is the right thing to do.
- *Obedience:* A discipline that sheds light on the hidden things of God.
- *Obedience:* One step toward God that's worth more than years of studying the subject.
- *Obedience:* When believers who hear the promises of God give equal heed to obeying the commands of God.
- *Obedience:* The most effective prescription for spiritual health.
- *Obedience:* An act of worship that removes pretense from our prayers.

William Booth, founder of The Salvation Army, is on record as saying, "Go and get sure about God, and then you will have no difficulty in obeying Him—only get a proper idea of God, and you will be frightened enough of disobeying so great, and powerful, and holy a Being. . . . Obedience is only another word for the active side of religion."

Prayer and fasting lead to a life of obedience. It is not about us getting our way or making our claim. No, it is about something a whole lot deeper and a great deal more profitable. Prayer and fasting lead us to see a breakthrough in the area of disobedience into the light of walking in obedience to God. God does respond to a heart that desires more than anything to please Him.

On July 20, 1976, the *Viking I* spacecraft touched down on the surface of Mars. Programmed to work until 1994, it pleased scientists by performing beautifully, sending back information whenever it was asked—that is, until November 19, 1982. On that day the *Viking* flight team at the Jet Propulsion Laboratory in Pasadena, California, radioed instructions to the spacecraft's computer, expecting an appropriate response. But no answer came. The *uplinked* message from Earth was not acknowledged, and no *downlink* reply was ever given. Despite concentrated efforts by a team of experts, the spacecraft remains silent. No one knows whether it will ever respond to Earth's signals again.

As followers of Jesus, we have the assurance that our *uplink* prayer messages to God will never have that problem. We will never need to get on the phone and complain, "Heaven, we have a problem."

When we pray and fast, our prayers are heard. As God purifies the motives and sensitizes the heart, He is drawn to us in our weaknesses. When our hearts are right before the Father, the purity of our communications will never go unheeded, nor will He ever fail to respond to our deepest needs. This is when spiritual breakthroughs occur. This is the nature of God. He desires to know us, to work with us, to refine us, and to be pleased with who we are and what we do. In turn He wants us to love Him, serve Him, live for Him, and to surrender fully to Him.

REFLECTION QUESTIONS

1. Do you struggle with being obedient to God? If so, why?

2. Which one of the seven principles mentioned in this chapter do you need the most in your life right now?

3. What is the last specific prayer God answered for you?

For me, living is Christ and dying is gain.
—Philippians 1:21

*Now praise the L*ORD*, all you servants of the L*ORD *who stand
in the L*ORD*'s house at night! Lift up your hands in the holy
place, and praise the L*ORD*!*
—Psalm 134:1–2

*For I am already being poured out as a drink offering, and
the time for my departure is close.*
—2 Timothy 4:6

Chapter Five
Surrendering Fully to God

When I write the words, "surrendering fully to God," I think
of the apostle Paul. From the moment he was radically converted to Jesus Christ, he became a prime example of absolute surrender. From that moment all the way to his death,
he poured out his life for Jesus and the gospel of Jesus Christ.
The last letter he wrote before his death was to Timothy.

We refer to that letter as being 2 Timothy. Paul was in
prison in Rome. Chatter must have filled the region that this
time Paul was never going to leave prison alive. Even Paul

knew that his time for death was at hand. However, whether through his life or even through his death, he was going to live a surrendered life to God.

This time Paul knew he would not be rescued from a lion's mouth or from the devastation of a stoning, but he would face death. At some point, just before AD 68 when Nero stopped reigning in Rome, Paul was escorted to his death. He was beheaded for Jesus Christ.

In 2 Timothy 4:6 we read some powerful words Paul penned to Timothy that God wanted us to have as well: "For I am already being poured out as a drink offering, and the time for my departure is close." This word pictures a life surrendered fully to God. Let me explain.

Paul picks up on some Old Testament language, referring to being "poured out as a drink offering." The drink offering was poured out on the altar after the burnt offering was given. Paul was saying, "I am that offering." Urgency and finality rang loud and clear through that declaration. I believe Paul was saying, "I am pouring myself out slowly, and I willingly will shed my blood as a way to give myself all to God, even in death." Paul was moving toward his death, and he knew it.

He refers to his departure, meaning he was about to be killed for Jesus Christ. This word "departure" gives us two word pictures. Its usage illustrates a ship lifting its anchor to leave. Its usage also illustrates soldiers who were breaking their camp. Both word pictures illustrate *going home.* In other words Paul was informing us that he was setting sail for eternity and he was taking down the tent, preparing to go home to be with Jesus.

This is why earlier in his life he penned Philippians 1:21, "For me, living is Christ, and dying is gain." You see, Paul did not see himself losing either way. Living on this earth, all for Jesus! Dying for Christ, all for Jesus! Giving his life in death was gain!

Paul did not see himself sacrificing his life once and for all for the gospel of Jesus Christ, nor did he see it as Nero taking his life. Paul was convinced that he was giving his life away to Jesus and the gospel even in his death. Paul was willing to shed his blood as a way to give himself to God, even in his death. Without any question at all, he was a man who was surrendered fully to God. Paul's life testified at all times, even in his death, "I am pouring myself out to Jesus."

Let's fast-forward to the late 1800s: Billy Sunday was a man who understood living a life surrendered to God fully. Sunday understood, if there is to be an outpouring of God's Spirit in our personal lives, in our churches, and in our nation, then there will be a continual denial of self and full surrender to God. Until our minds and wills are called into order by the Spirit of God, they will remain open to every foreign idea, every theological aberration, and the acceptance of virtually anything that feels good, looks good, takes virtually no commitment, and has drive-in convenience. None of this will move us closer to God and into His presence.

Only when we lift our hands to the Father in full surrender to His will can we understand even remotely what

God wants to do in our lives. As we enter God's gateway to the supernatural, one of the most immediate messages we will receive from our holy God is, "My son, my daughter, are you prepared to surrender it all? Are you willing to pour yourself out to Me completely? To give up your shallow lives for an experience that will touch your heart for eternity? I will not tell you where I will have you go. I just want to know if you are prepared to surrender your life to Me. Each morning when you awake, I will be with you to help you and guide you through your day. But my question remains: As you do your daily duties, will you surrender it all . . . to Me?" Paul understood this and so did America's most influential evangelist in the first two decades of the nineteenth century. Spiritual breakthroughs are ours when we surrender our lives fully to God.

WHAT IS REVIVAL?

Until we make a decision to deal honestly with God's questions about full allegiance to Him, there will be little or no prospect of an awakening in our hearts, no stirring of the Spirit in our churches, and no revival in our land. True revival is nothing less or more than the manifested presence of God in our lives. It is when Jesus is free to be who He wants to be in, through, and around us.

One of the greatest secrets to get us to this point is prayer and fasting. It opens the heart to God fully. Revival comes when we give ourselves to God completely. Revival is the manifested presence of God in our lives.

Are there other words and phrases we would rather use, perhaps, instead of *surrender, commitment, compelling vision?* Could it be we've not seen an all-out awakening because individual believers and our church leaders have failed to set themselves apart and in humility and desperation surrender themselves fully to God?

The Scripture tells us that without a vision the people die. They die in spirit, in their influence, in right decision making, in their zeal to share their faith with neighbors; and they die in their desire to bring closure to the Great Commission by keeping the gospel neat and tidy, homogenized and pasteurized, so there's no way a lost world could know of the unwrapped gift that awaits them. Until the church of Jesus Christ regains its spiritual power, recaptures its spiritual passion, is willing to pay the price, and begins to demonstrate an unfailing love for Jesus Christ, it will remain cold, out of touch, ineffective, purposeless, nonproductive, ingrown, and something so tepid that the only sensible thing to do is to spit it out.

Harsh words, but this is where we are. Only an outpouring of God's Spirit that leads to revival will do. Revival begins with you and me. It starts with me. I must live fully surrendered to Jesus, always pouring myself out to Him.

A SPIRITUAL BREAKTHROUGH AWAITS YOU

A spiritual breakthrough is the result when we surrender ourselves fully to God, transferring all ownership to the one true Owner, Jesus Christ. We do not need to grab but to release. We do not live with our hands in fists, but with our hands open. We will never choose to let God have His way with us if we continue to hang on to our own desires, our own dreams, and our own bondage. In wartime, if we are captured by an enemy, we are commanded to surrender. At that moment we have a choice. We can take our chances, make a run for it, and hope for the best. But if an armed enemy pursues us, we have little chance of physical survival. When God asks us to surrender to Him, the analogy is the same except for one key point: God is not the enemy. He is our Father and our Friend. He knows what's best for us. That's why He wants us to surrender our minds to Him (the way we think); our wills (what we're convinced we should be or do); our emotions (how we feel); our bodies (the sum of who we are); our talents (the abilities for which we often take full credit); our attitudes (our often selfish responses to others); our motives (what we know really drives us to succeed); our careers (the business of life that too often becomes our own life).

Personally I do not know of a better way to experience this fully surrendered life than through the gateway of prayer and fasting. When we surrender, we *transfer all ownership to the one true Owner, Jesus Christ.* We exchange our lives for His life! And when we enter God's gateway to supernatural power for living, we begin to learn what *an exchanged life* is all about. When we fast and pray, we may become influenced by God's character. We may hear Him speak to us in a voice we've never heard before. It's not a harsh voice, but rather the voice of a waiting Father who will always tell us the truth. Whenever God calls me to fast, where I deny myself the natural act of eating to focus on specific spiritual goals, I ask God to show me those areas in my life that I'm still keeping for Ronnie Floyd, asking, "God, what am I still not surrendering fully to you? Show me. I cannot see the blind spots in my life without your divine counsel."

Andrew Murray writes in his sermon *Absolute Surrender,* that God is . . .

> the Fountain of life, the only Source of existence and power and goodness, and throughout the universe there is nothing good but what God works. God has created the sun and the moon and the stars and the flowers and the trees and the grass; and are they not all absolutely surrendered to God? Do they not allow God to work in them just what He pleases? When God clothes the lily with its beauty, is it not yielded up, surrendered, given over to God as He works in its beauty? And God's redeemed children . . . can you think that God can work His work if there is only half or a part of them surrendered? God cannot do it. God is life and love and blessing and power and infinite beauty, and God delights to communicate Himself to every child who is prepared to receive Him. This one lack of absolute surrender is just the thing that hinders God. And now He comes, as God. He claims it.[1]

Release it all to Jesus. Pour yourself out to Jesus. Hold nothing back. Surrender it all. Everything.

A SHORT SEASON WITH LONG-TERM EFFECT

Does a life of full surrender to God have its challenges? Yes, it does. The challenges and difficulties will be so overwhelming at times that we may want to retreat to our old ways of shaping our own destinies and running our own lives. That's why once we enter God's gateway to supernatural power we must never leave His presence. Fasting may be a temporal activity—a few days or forty days—but the significance and the effect of our fast and time with God is meant to last.

When asked if this full surrender is even possible, Andrew Murray responded, "What has God promised you, and what can God do to fill a vessel absolutely surrendered to Him? God wants to bless you in a way beyond what you expect. From the beginning, ear hath not heard, neither hath the eye seen what God hath prepared for them that wait for Him. God has prepared unheard of things you never can think of: blessings much more wonderful than you can imagine, more mighty than you can conceive. They are divine blessings."[2]

If our lives are not receptive to the things of God, if it's business is usual, if our tempers rule us, our emotions control us, our minds deceive us, and our hearts are not warm to the God who loves us, I suggest that surrender to God has not yet become a viable activity in our lives. If that is the case, then our Christian walks will be most difficult assignments, bordering on confusion and drudgery, because we shall be wearing masks, playing charades, pretending to be one thing but, in truth, being quite the opposite. We fool only ourselves, and with each sleight of heart, we put more distance between ourselves and the God who loves us. We remain miserable when we depend on our own talents and make our own plans, becoming even more distressed when we then ask God to bless our efforts, knowing He had no part in them.

When someone asked William Booth, founder of The Salvation Army, the secret of his enormous success, Booth remained silent for several moments. Finally, with tear-filled eyes, he said, "There have been men with greater brains or opportunities than I, but I made up my mind that God would have all of William Booth there was."[3]

Several years later when General Booth's daughter heard about her father's comment regarding his full surrender to God, she said, "That wasn't really his secret—his secret was that he never took it back."[4]

And that's the secret we need to discover: We may never be a William Booth, but all of us can, in response to God's grace and mercy in saving us, give Him our all and never take it back. There is also a practical side to surrendering fully to God: our burdens become His, not ours. Finally we start to place our frustrations and worries where we once only laid our sins. We develop a spiritually healthy perspective on what was once a terrible frustration with life and its inconsistencies because we now no longer must carry the burden. Once filled with dark, foreboding thoughts, we now are free to be the people God created us to be because He has cast out those terrible demons of fear, anxiety, codependence, having to be number one, attitudes that hurt, and actions that are unkind. As we go into that quiet place to meet God in fasting and prayer, our souls are focused on Him alone, and therein lies the difference. We become oblivious to the noise of life when we are in His presence. Life's babble is set aside as we throw ourselves at the feet of our Savior. It's only in the presence of our heavenly Father that we hear His call to full surrender.

Prayer and fasting can lead you into this kind of surrender. This short season of fasting, whether one day or forty days, does something you cannot do. It does something only God can do. It sets the heart free, opens the hands to release, and positions you to hear the voice of God like never before. It is one short season that will have long-term effect upon your life. It almost seems as if God is attracted to one who prays and fasts.

God Is Attracted to Weakness

Surrendering to God is abandoning all that we have, to receive all that God possesses. It is not the skills, talents, and gifts that God places in our hands that matter; it is the full, complete, unequivocal surrender of those meager abilities to Him that He uses to do great things in our lives. In his wonderful book *Fresh Wind, Fresh Fire*, Jim Cymbala, pastor of the

Brooklyn Tabernacle Church in Brooklyn, New York, wrote: "I discovered an astonishing truth; *God is attracted to weakness.* He can't resist those who humbly and honestly admit how desperately they need him. The first step in any spiritual awakening is demolition. We cannot make headway in seeking God without first tearing down the accumulated junk in our souls. Rationalizing has to cease. We have to start seeing the sinful debris we hadn't noticed before, which is what holds back the blessing of God. Sin grieves the Holy Spirit and quenches His power among us."[5]

Prayer and fasting make the spirit and heart tender before God. We begin to see things like never before. We see sins we have never noticed before. Prayer and fasting make us weak physically but strong spiritually. I believe God is attracted to the weakness that comes to those who pray and fast.

Some years ago I had the privilege to preach at the Brooklyn Tabernacle Church and pray one day I can do it again. It was a thrilling experience because I saw a church that personified this truth. Their weakness was a magnet to the mighty manifested presence of God. These surrendered Christ followers and their surrendered pastor were recipients of an unusual manifestation of God's Spirit. His presence is real among them. Their absolute surrender to Jesus was amazing.

Surrender means we must be emptied before we can be filled. We must die to live; give it all up to gain. No great work anywhere by anyone at any time has ever come about without surrender. For His kingdom to come, our kingdom must go.

In the words of Flora Larsson from *My Treasure Chest* . . .

> Have it Your own way, Lord,
> You've won!
> I lay my weapons down.
> You would not give me blow for blow,
> No steel met mine,
> And yet I am vanquished.[6]

When we surrender to God, we become better fathers, better mothers, better husbands, and better wives, better children, better students, better employees, better leaders because we have transferred our lives, our ideas, our best-laid plans over to our heavenly Father. It's the transfer of our bodies (all we are), our minds (how we think), our spirits (where God lives), our tongues (every word we utter), our attitudes (the way we *respond* to others), and our motives (the reality of who we are). All that God has given us we must transfer, give over, *surrender* to Him for His great purposes, and no longer keep them for our own. The more we live in God's holy presence, staying focused on Him through the joys of the disciplines of fasting and prayer, the more we will learn of His character; and that's what we must desire more than life itself.

No one has ever *made* more promises than God, no one has ever *kept* more promises than God, and no one has ever been more *faithful* than God. God will be faithful to answer all His promises to those who pray and fast. He knows that we are engaged in the battle of our lives because He has already told us: "For our struggle is not against flesh and blood, but against the rulers, against the authorities, against the powers of this dark world and against the spiritual forces of evil in the heavenly realms. Therefore put on the full armor of God, so that when the day of evil comes, you may be able to stand your ground, and after you have done everything, to stand" (Eph. 6:12–13 NIV). When we pray and fast, walking in the power of our weaknesses, strengthened by a Holy powerful God, we will face intense spiritual warfare. Yet we will win because we are surrendered fully to Jesus.

THE GLORY

Think on these words for a moment. I believe you will be encouraged.

The glory of these forty days we celebrate with songs of praise; for Christ through whom all things were made, himself has fasted and has prayed.

Alone and fasting Moses saw the loving God who gave the law; and to Elijah, fasting, came the steeds and chariots of flame. So Daniel trained his mystic sight, delivered from the lions' might; and John, the Bridegroom's friend, became the herald of Messiah's name.

Then grant us, Lord, like them to be full oft in fast and prayer with thee; our spirits strength with thy grace, and give us joy to see thy face. Father, Son, and Spirit blest, to thee be every prayer addressed, who art in threefold Name adored, from age to age, the only Lord.[7]

Whether forty days, fourteen days, one or two days, or one day each month—whenever we come into the presence of our living God in fasting and prayer will be a glorious experience. What may have been a perfunctory "I promise to love You, and serve You, Jesus" prayer in the past is now transformed from the dull routine of vain repetition to one of adoration, praise, confession, and thanksgiving as we present ourselves humbly before the King of kings, asking Him to direct our steps, control our thoughts, and warm our hearts. Once hastily spoken, and perhaps even bordering on the insincere, our more thoughtful promises to God now take on new significance: Our promises to be kinder, more loving, more in control of our tempers, more effective in our witness, better fathers, mothers, husbands, and wives echo in the purity of His presence.

Will You Join the Fasting Team?

Are the spiritual disciplines of fasting and praying important enough for you to join the team? Are prayer and fasting mandatory? I'll answer this question with another question. If we wanted to become tennis players, would it be possible for us to participate in the game without hitting the ball and running to get the ball to return it? Some action must take place if we are to be *in the game*. Those who choose not to play the game are called spectators, onlookers, involved to a degree but only on the periphery and away from the action.

There's nothing wrong with being spectators—that is, *unless* they sit idly in the stands and watch only because they have not yet been informed that they, too, have been invited to play. God will not coax us to accept the conditions necessary to enjoy the supernatural power He promises will be ours through fasting and prayer. But He has issued an invitation to what promises to be the experience of our lives. Fasting-and-prayer seasons are for reflection, celebration, and gratitude carried out in a spirit of quietness—an unseen, unnoticed activity, kept from the prying eyes of others, an experience to be enjoyed alone with God. This verse sets the tone for any fast we might undertake:

> Whenever you fast, don't be sad-faced like the hypocrites. For they make their faces unattractive so their fasting is obvious to people. I assure you: They've got their reward! But when you fast, put oil on your head, and wash your face, so that you don't show your fasting to people but to your Father who is in secret. And your Father who sees in secret will reward you. (Matt. 6:16–18)

The Lord is calling you to join the fasting team. It is a team in great need for players, not spectators. The church must get out of the stands and onto the field. These are critical moments in American history, and they deserve urgent action. *The time is now* for us to stand up humbly, surrendering to Jesus fully, pouring ourselves out to Him completely, in prayer and fasting.

A. W. Tozer wrote, "True Christian joy is the heart's harmonious response to the Lord's song of love."[8] That song of love includes the poetry of fasting and prayer, God-ordained vehicles to put us in the presence of our heavenly Father in a way we otherwise may never have known Him. The song that provides spiritual breakthroughs coming no other way except through prayer and fasting, even those breakthroughs needed to help you face your future.

REFLECTION QUESTIONS

1. Would you consider yourself fully surrendered to God?

2. What keeps you from surrendering to God fully?

3. When was the last time you believe you were fully surrendered to God?

"For I know the plans I have for you"—this is the LORD's declaration—"plans for your welfare, not for disaster, to give you a future and a hope. You will call to Me and come and pray to Me, and I will listen to you. You will seek Me and find Me when you search for Me with all your heart. I will be found by you."
—Jeremiah 29:11–14

What then are we to say about these things? If God is for us, who is against us?
—Romans 8:31

Chapter Six

Facing the Future Boldly with God

One of the most thrilling opportunities I have ever had in my life is when Dr. Bill Bright invited me to Fort Collins, Colorado, for the purpose of preaching to thousands of their leaders from across the world. I remember seeing him in his hotel room just hours before I was to speak, and he said to me, "Ronnie, challenge them to fast and pray for the nation they are serving." I told him that was exactly what I was going to do.

I remember walking into an arena located on the campus of Colorado State University. The arena was packed with thousands of ministers, evangelists, and missionaries who were connected to the phenomenal ministry, Campus Crusade for Christ.

When I stood up to preach God's Word, I challenged them to pray and fast for their nation, the nation they are serving for the purpose of winning people to Christ. It was a powerful experience for me personally, and I know from reports sent to me later that it seemed to be a powerful visionary experience for those who were present.

I remember seeing people who were in that experience that day, and they informed me they did just what they felt God was calling them to do: *pray and fast for forty days for their nation, the nation they were serving to win to Christ.* These missionaries, ministers, evangelists—Christians—were all trying to engage their future ministries in their respective countries. They were there for the purpose of being launched out to their future.

Through the calling of God, it was apparent in that meeting, that God wanted to do a new thing in the future of those leaders.

The Spirit's call to pray and fast for their nation radically altered their agenda but strengthened it with great depth. I am convinced, some by testimonies back to me and then just knowing God does powerful things in the lives and ministries of those who fast, that the Lord was calling every one of us, including me, to a new future!

A few years later I was in Thailand in an annual meeting of missionaries supported by the Southern Baptist Convention, who served the nations of China, Taiwan, and others in that part of the world; and the Lord instructed me to preach on prayer and fasting, calling them to pray and fast for the nation and the specific people group they were serving with the goal of winning them to Jesus. Fewer than one thousand people were in that setting, but what a powerful setting as those godly, hungry missionaries made commitments to God to do just that. These men and women of God are a part of a spiritual force of fifty-five hundred missionaries of the International Mission Board of the Southern Baptist Convention. Due to the heart of the churches affiliated with this denomination, the International Mission Board has missionaries serving in almost every country of the world. It is a fabulous missionary force because many of them are committed to biblical principles like prayer and fasting.

Can you imagine what it would be like to be in a strange culture? A culture that you do not understand and even have a hard time communicating in it? I would imagine after a few weeks, perhaps just days, the missionary would have to come to the end of himself as he thought about the future. *Therefore, all he has left is God.* Hey, that is not a bad place to be; its a great place to be.

When it is "all on God," we are strong. When coupled with prayer and fasting, we who are weak become strong, very strong.

The result: we are facing the future boldly with God! When we come to the end of ourselves, God is ready to step in powerfully and supernaturally with spiritual breakthroughs. You see, just as these missionaries know, without the God dynamic involved, we can accomplish little to nothing.

FACING THE FUTURE WITH PRAYER AND FASTING

Fasting is abstaining from food with a spiritual goal in mind. It is when you neglect the most powerful lust within you, which is for food, in order to pursue an in-depth, intimate, personal relationship with Jesus Christ. I am convinced there is a correlation in Scripture with humility and fasting and prayer. When I share with you about facing your future with prayer and fasting, what does all that mean?

Facing the Future with Humility

First Peter 5:6 says, "*Humble yourselves* therefore under the mighty hand of God, so that He may exalt you in due time" (italics added). As we have mentioned already, we are instructed to take the initiative ourselves to humble ourselves before God. The responsibility is on us to humble ourselves. This call from God concerning humility means that we are to lay ourselves low before God, to become insignificant and weak before God. Within the context of the entire Scripture, I believe we do that through prayer and fasting.

A decision to fast is a decision to humble yourself before God. If you want to face your future boldly, nothing creates holy, humble boldness more than prayer and fasting.

Biblically there is precedence in this. Experientially I am confident it is right.

When I go through a season of prayer and fasting, I gain a holy, humble boldness when I engage the future in any way. It does not matter what is before me, God moves so powerfully in me, I am filled with confidence, God confidence.

A. W. Tozer said the following about humility: "Humility is as scarce as an albino robin."[1] How many albino robins have you ever seen in your life? Probably none! In our American culture, humility and seeking God in prayer and fasting are rare.

Facing the Future in Desperation

Ezra 8:21–23 says, *"I proclaimed a fast* by the Ahava River, *so that we might humble ourselves* before our God and *ask Him for a safe journey for us*, our children, and all our possessions. I did this because I was ashamed to ask the king for infantry and cavalry to protect us from enemies during the journey, since we had told him, 'The hand of our God is gracious to all who seek Him, but His great anger is against all who abandon Him.' *So we fasted and pleaded with our God* about this, and *He granted our request"* (italics added).

Desperation is not bad. In fact, I believe God creates it at times within our hearts and lives. Desperation is not bad when you are desperate for God to move mightily in a situation. When we get desperate enough, we will take radical action in our lives.

Ezra did this. He had testified to the king of how powerful His God was, but then, when he had the people near the Ahava River in enemy territory, he just felt it was a poor testimony to ask the king for infantry and cavalry to protect his people.

Therefore Ezra called the people to fast. His desperation for God's name to be lifted up and for the enemies to be defeated without man's help motivated him to call for this fast.

Why did he do this? He did this so the people would humble themselves before God. *Desperation for God to move coupled with humbling ourselves before God is a winning combination!* Prayer and fasting brings that winning combination to the forefront. When we fast, we humble ourselves before God. When we are desperate for God to do something as was Ezra, we fast and pray, making our request to God.

The people fasted and pleaded with God, and He miraculously granted their request for safety. He heard their requests. He was attracted to their weakness. God wanted to demonstrate Himself miraculously. Guess what—He did!

I want to challenge you to face your future with a desperation for God to work in your life. When desperation is alive in your heart, pray and fast. God has you in that mode so you will pursue Him with all of your heart. Just as David humbled his soul in fasting, as recorded in Psalm 35:13, we need to humble ourselves in fasting, especially when a desperation is alive within us, for God to do a mighty, fresh, new work.

Facing the Future against All Odds

The drama recorded in 2 Chronicles 20 speaks of how King Jehoshaphat proclaimed a fast so that the people would seek the Lord for guidance, direction, and, most of all, protection. As they were surrounded by their enemies, God was moved by their fasting and saved them in dramatic fashion. As we have already talked of the story in this book, I just want to remind you that God's people did not have any hope at all in that setting.

However, *against all odds*, they prayed and fasted, requesting God to move miraculously. God answered their prayer and did just that. He saved them by God's mighty power. They needed a breakthrough and God gave them one!

When you are up against all odds, pray and fast. Do not shy away when the circumstances seem hopeless. That is exactly the kind of situation God loves to move in among us. Take Nehemiah, he faced a hopeless situation in Jerusalem, but through prayer and fasting, God gave him a God-sized vision and moved in a God-sized way. Even when you are *against all odds*, He will do the same for you. He will do the same for me. He will do the same for America. He will do the same for your business. He will do the same for your church.

How exciting is this? You have the privilege to face your future with prayer and fasting, even against all odds.

Facing the Future with Good Company

King David fasted. God filled him with hope. Jonah fasted. God gave Nineveh a revival. John the Baptist fasted. He preached with power and fire! Jesus fasted. Everywhere He went and everyone He touched were never same. The apostle Paul fasted. No one, other than Jesus, had a greater influence on the church of Jesus Christ not only in his generation but in the generations following.

What more do I need to say? If fasting and prayer were good enough for these men, how can you walk away from them? You cannot biblically or personally dismiss prayer and fasting. God calls everyone to practice prayer and fasting. He calls us to do them in different ways and for different times. The issues are not how long, or should I, but when. God wants us to pray and fast.

Facing the Future with Power

After the Mount of Transfiguration occurred, the disciples had an opportunity to deliver a person from a demon. I just imagine they tried to do it as they had seen Jesus do it. Yet it did not work!

As the story is recorded in Matthew 17, Jesus told them that if they wanted to move mountains, they would have to believe. Then He shared with them that demonic forces and major obstacles cannot be overcome without prayer and fasting! What an incredible statement.

Special power for a specific need comes only through prayer and fasting. What a superb statement and reality taught to us through Jesus' life.

Therefore, when we pray and fast, we face the future with power, supernatural power! God empowers us to do great things when we pray and fast.

I challenge you right now: face your future with God's power! It is yours as you pray and fast. God can do more in a moment than you can do in a lifetime! Believe it. Practice it.

Begin it. Do it!

In 1996 I was on James Dobson's *Focus on the Family* broadcast. He was interviewing me about prayer and fasting. I had that interview transcribed to share with you a few statements I made then that I still believe today. He asked me that day, "Did He reward you with His presence during that time?" I responded in 1996 to this question saying:

> Like never before. There is nothing that happens any greater than when you pray and fast than to be aware of the incredible presence of God. The holiness of God comes to be more real than ever before, and the exceeding sinfulness of your own life is revealed. God did some things in me that needed to be done. I was a proud, arrogant pastor, and I needed God to break me, and to mold me, and to give me a fresh anointing where I would love people the way I needed to love them. Be the man of God I needed to be. Be the daddy I needed to be. Be the husband I

needed to be. By no means am I there, but I guarantee it, I'm a lot further along in that journey.[2]

Friends, I have prayed and fasted with consistency numerous times for numerous years. I promise you, what I said in 1996 was true in that interview. There is not a time when God's presence is more evident in my life than when I pray and fast.

When you pray and fast, the powerful presence of God will accompany you and wake up in you like never before. You will never be the same—never.

THE PRICE

Will you pay the price? Who will be that man? Who will be that woman? Will it be you? Will it be me? How will we know if God has put His divine hand on us to be part of this massive outpouring of His Spirit in our time? Again, I say the only way I know that we'll be quiet and attentive enough to hear God's voice is through the godly disciplines of fasting and prayer. Only when we experience the depth of God and His love will we be able to rise to newness of life. But it will be necessary to pay the price, just as we will always pay a price for something that is lasting and worthwhile. Paying the price will cost us some conveniences.

To fast means to deny ourselves what is common, normal, and necessary—food—for a period of time so that our minds will become sharp, our hearts softened, and our spirits receptive to what God has to say to us. The price is great but worth it. Why? God promises to fill the void that the absence of food creates; He will pour out His blessings and sate us in a way that food neither can nor will. Without this intentional, heightened spiritual focus that comes from humbling ourselves in God's presence, we will be doomed to face the future timidly, defensively, without power, and without serious motivation. But when we have been in the presence of Almighty God and have taken our directions from His heart, we will have the wherewithal, the strength, the desire, the courage, and the confidence to face the future boldly, without fear, and without compromise.

WHEN SOMEONE PAYS THE PRICE

I always stand amazed at what happens when people pay the price to fast and pray for their families, or situations, or our nation, or their church. Testimonies have blessed me through the years that come from so many people who have implemented these kinds of prayer and fasting principles into their lives.

One of my sweet friends in the Lord is a lady named Margo Mason who attends our Pinnacle Hills Campus. She is a *radical football fan* and believes there is no other team than the Fighting Irish of the University of Notre Dame. One Sunday morning when I was speaking, after Notre Dame had gone through major upheaval in their national coaching search, I popped off: "I just want to notify everyone, if the University of Notre Dame calls me and offers me their head football coach position, I am out of here!" Due to the major national attention of their search that had turned sour, I added that brief word. When I was greeting people after church that day, Margo informed me seriously, "If you really desire to go be the coach at Notre Dame, my brother is the associate athletic director, and I will tell him." She caught me by surprise, which led to laughter and eventually a sweet, close relationship with her and her husband, Richard, who are both great warriors in prayer.

Due to matters in her life and some situations in her family, prayer and fasting have become part of Margo's life. She shared with me recently, and I requested that she write me a testimony.

You see, as you read this, you learn what happens when someone pays the price in prayer and fasting. Margo stated:

> Through prayer and fasting God began to restore my family after sin and deception ripped through like a tornado setting out to destroy everyone in its path. Fasting brought me to a higher level of spiritual growth. God began to open my spiritual eyes to things I never saw before in my own life such as how weak and frail I really am. My sufficiency comes from Him, and He controls it all. Jesus gave me a clear understanding of what it was totally to forgive and gave me the opportunity to do that, strengthening me to walk the journey He had planned for me before I ever breathed my first breath. Prayer and fasting gave me courage to play the role Christ wanted me to play to members of my family, which was to walk in truth no matter what the cost or the

outcome. He gave me a voice to speak into the lives of my family who were suffering from hurt, pain, and anger and to lovingly lead them back to the feet of Jesus as we prayed together.

I asked God in my times of prayer and fasting to restore our family, but God was not interested in taking this broken family and restoring it back to what it was. His desires were far greater than mine. . . . His desire was to grow us beyond ourselves to look more like Him and less like us, to prepare us for eternity where we will be the bride of Christ equally yoked . . . which comes through suffering. Prayer and fasting were and are the means by which this happened and is happening. *My communication with God through prayer and fasting may not change my circumstances, but they will change my heart, enable me to see my situation from His perspective, grow my faith, and trust Him in all for all.*

What an incredible testimony. Due to Margo's paying the price in prayer and fasting about the future of her family, God worked in her first. He dealt with her attitude, changing it and leading her to understand forgiveness in a new way. Change began happening in the family, but that change was not a return to the past. It became an entrée into a new future that God would now create among the players in that family. For Margo, prayer and fasting resulted in some major spiritual breakthroughs in her personally, in her family, and in life situations.

Read her last sentence again. Powerful. Insightful. God changes us when we pray and fast. It is not about the circumstances lining up to our preferences or desires. However, through prayer and fasting God works so powerfully within us, our hearts change so much. What matters most is one thing: the Lord's will. We gain perspective we have never had and enter into a level of faith and trust that cannot and will not occur without prayer and fasting happening in our lives.

As you join us into the journey of prayer and fasting, remember, the future is not to be feared. God will do such a work in you, as he did in Margo, as He has done in me numerous times, that you can face your future boldly with God. Do not wait. Enter in.

Write Down What God Does

On January 1, 1990, I began writing a one-page prayer to God daily. That written prayer occurs at the end of my prayer and Bible reading time. Sure, some days it is more than just a page, but it serves as a point of focus about what is on my heart on that day specifically. It now serves as documentation for my spiritual life. I write down what God has on my heart and what God is doing in my life. It is the story God has created in me all these years.

Well, when you step out and enter into times of prayer and fasting, write down what God does in you. Journaling. Whether you like that term or not or prefer another one, just keep it simple: write down what God says to you and does within you.

When I enter into a time of prayer and fasting, especially for seven days or more, I write down what God says to me and does within me in a different journal. I have major records of various things, volumes of Scriptures and prayers, hopes and dreams, recorded in those journals.

Before I Go on a Long-term Fast

Before I go on a long-term fast, I ask God to give me His plan that He wants me to pray through or about during those days. These things become my prayer list that I take to God daily while praying and fasting. It gives me focus, direction, and as God directs me, I add to that list. Additionally, when God answers, if He does in the time of fasting, I record it as answered.

Before you go on a long-term fast, get God's heart on why you are going on this journey and what you need to trust Him for. Remember, fasting is abstinence from food *with a spiritual goal in mind*. This spiritual goal or goals is the list you have created under the leadership of God to pray about and through daily.

Take the time to write it down so you will have clear and specific direction for your journey. It becomes your spiritual navigation system for this prayer and fasting journey.

While on a Long-term Fast

While on a long-term fast, spend time alone with God. I usually spend at least the first hour of each day with God in my normal schedule. When I pray and fast, I may end up spending at least two hours per day and usually more. Why?

Focus is greater when you pray and fast. As you focus, retreat at least during one meal to be alone and meet with God. Read His Word. Present your list again. Listen to what God is saying to you. Write it down. Record what God is saying to you and doing within you, the things He is putting into your heart.

The following is just an example of what I wrote one morning while on a forty-day fast:

> I pray and fast at this time for the purpose of humbling myself before You, to be in continual touch with You, to experience the immediacy of Your presence, and to receive the authority of Jesus in my life. As a minister of the Lord, may I stand in the gap for my nation and God. May the Holy Spirit be my power and my authority. May my heart be broken as I give it to You. May God withhold His judgment and pour out His Spirit on all mankind.
>
> I pray today that I will be Your man. Not man's man, not almighty man, but God's man. I pray I will do all and be all God wants me to be and do. May the Lord be God upon me today. May my soul pant for Thee, my God. May I thirst for You, O my

living God. Even as I fast from food, may I have an appetite to be with You and allow You to nourish me with Yourself.

Anoint me with the oil of Jesus' joy. O God, speak to me. In Jesus' name, speak to me. Be glorified in me. I need Your Word. My trust is in You, O God. I pray for God to do more in a moment today than I could ever do in a lifetime. O God, give me Your passion and Your heart. May I simply be Your representative today and every day.

To You alone be the praise for guiding and strengthening me during this forty-day fast. O God, I pray for the hand of my God to be upon me. I praise You for the affirmation of James 4:10, "Humble yourselves in the presence of the Lord, and He will exalt you" (NASB). O God, You have given a greater grace to those who humble themselves before Your holy face.

Fill me with the fire of the Spirit and the joy of the Lord. I ask that Your power be upon me. Let me be an instrument of God to see people released from physical, emotional, and spiritual bondage, both at home and throughout the world. Thank You God for these forty days. I give them—and all that comes out of them—to the glory of Jesus. May this be only the beginning of a new life and walk with You.

Again, this is just one example of what I wrote on a given morning on a forty-day fast. Each day is different. The principle is *not to do what I do* but simply to write down what God is saying to you and doing within your life.

Your Last Moments on a Long-term Fast

Your last moments on a long-term fast are so important. They are so significant that I usually retreat for at least the last twenty-four hours of that time. I go into a local hotel or somewhere by myself. While there I open my heart one last time before God, sell out one more time to Him, listen to Him intently, and I write down what He says to me through His Word.

In those last hours I read my journal of what God has said to me. While I do so, I highlight the most significant things. Following this, I then reread the highlights. Then I write down the final lessons I feel God has taught me and even those things I believe God is going to do. These would be my takeaways. Most, if not all of those, are on those highlighted areas.

This again provides focus and clarity about the future.

Clarity in life is imperative. Prayer and fasting can bring clarity.

After a Long-term Fast

After a long-term fast God may release you to share some of your journey. Ask Him about it. Ensure He is releasing you to do it.

Some would take a self-righteous view and state the importance of privacy saying, "We are to do all of this in private." While we fast, we do need to be private about our journey. But remember that after two of Moses' fasts were over, people found out about them because from those fasts we have the Ten Commandments. Somehow we know Jesus was on a forty-day fast. Somehow we know story after story in Scripture of what God did, so someone talked about what God did.

Therefore, you do what God puts in your heart to do. Just be humble about it, never boasting in anyone or anything other than Jesus. Remember, all for Him.

Oh, by the way, none of this would be possible to know personally or share with anyone if you do not write it down. Write down what God does in your life. Record in writing the spiritual breakthroughs God brings as you have prayed and fasted. You will never regret it. It is powerful, releasing, and energizing when you go back through it in the future. Reading about a breakthrough that happened before gives you greater faith knowing that, if God did that, He can do what may be a great challenge before you in your life. The practical discipline of writing down what the Lord is saying to you and doing within you will help you face the future boldly with God.

When God Moves

More than six hundred years before Christ was born, the prophet Isaiah predicted that Christ's work of service on the cross would result in His satisfaction at the resurrection. Isaiah wrote, "After the suffering of his soul, he will see the light and be satisfied; by his knowledge my righteous servant will justify many, and he will bear their iniquities" (Isa. 53:11 NIV). Again that word *satisfied*. Filled to overflowing. Complete. What can we learn from Christ's example?

Certainly we learn that service isn't going to be easy. There *will* be suffering of our souls. Service will not be convenient. For some it will mean pain, possibly even death. But if God directs us and gives us His strength, then our service will be satisfying. Martin Lloyd-Jones wrote, "When God acts, He can do more in a minute than man with his organizing can do in fifty years."[3] I would add, or in a lifetime!

When God calls us to fast and pray, we are connected with the only true Source for spiritual power and breakthroughs. We are linked to a God who cleanses our hearts and purifies our spirits. As He makes us clean, He removes the dissonance and static that have short-circuited our communion with God.

As we fast and pray, we sharpen our focus as God lifts our spirits. When we choose not to be sated—satisfied—with physical food during our fast, our heavenly Father satisfies us with the delight of His presence. At first it is all so new, so unexpected. Then He takes hold of our eager hearts and speaks as we've never heard Him before. Yes, when God moves, and He will move, He will do more in a moment than you can do in a lifetime.

The Secret to Greatness

What is the secret to greatness? Who is this mighty God? Jesus, the Son of God, proclaimed that the first will be last, that the weak are the strong, and that the foolish are wise. He says that the poor and lowly, not the proud, possess the kingdom of heaven. He declares that greatness in His sight will come only through service to Him. In Matthew 20:25–28, we read:

> Jesus called them together and said, "You know that the rulers of the Gentiles lord it over them, and their high officials exercise authority over them. Not so with you. Instead, whoever wants to become great among you must be your servant, and whoever wants to be first must be your slave—just as the Son of Man did not come to be served, but to serve, and to give his life as a ransom for many." (NIV)

The secret to greatness in the kingdom of God is neither power nor position. Greatness is being conformed to the image of Jesus Christ. If we want to identify with Jesus in His glory, we must also identify with Him in His humility. A true servant looks for legitimate needs to meet, whether at home or across the ocean, ministering to others with joy and understanding. But for us to stay the course, to know the supernatural power of God that leads to experiencing spiritual breakthroughs, and to be able to face the future boldly with confidence, demands that we be alert to the vehicles that give us immediate access to enormous power—the disciplines of prayer and fasting. And they are disciplines. Fasting and prayer do not come naturally. We will have to reorder our priorities, reschedule our commitments, and revise our minuscule, man-made plans to make the time to be in the presence of the Lord. That is what these Old Testament saints did as they took God seriously in their lives:

- Abraham rose early to stand before the Lord (see Gen. 19:27).
- Jacob rose early to worship the Lord (see Gen. 28:18).
- Hannah and Elkanah rose early to worship God (see 1 Sam. 1:9).
- Moses rose up early to give God's message to Pharaoh (see Exod. 8:20).
- Joshua rose up early to capture Jericho (see Josh. 6:12).
- Gideon rose up early to examine the fleece (see Judg. 6:38).

What are we willing to do to come into His holy presence? Are we willing . . .

- to close the book of complaints and open the book of God's praise?
- to ignore what we feel life owes us and think more about what we owe others?
- to cease our unforgiveness that leads to bitterness and just once and for all, let it go?
- to stop looking for friendship and start being a friend?

- to be content with the material things God has already given us and stop fretting about the things we do not have?
- to enjoy God's simple blessings and stop striving for the artificial pleasures of the day?
- to quit looking for someone to help us and begin devoting ourselves to a lifetime of service in helping others come to know our Savior?
- to see a spiritual awakening of a world, a nation, a community, and a church *starting in our hearts* and through fasting and prayer enter God's gateway to spiritual breakthroughs that are so needed for this revival and awakening to take place?

You may say, "But I'm just one person, only a flickering candle in a windy world that doesn't give its allegiance to Jesus. What can I do when I feel so alone, wondering if God can use me and my limited capacities?"

If you feel you're in the minority in your walk with God, you have suddenly put yourself in good biblical company:

- When **Noah** was building the ark, he was very much in the minority, but he followed his Creator, and God blessed Noah and his family.
- When **Joseph** was sold into Egypt by his brothers, he was in the minority, and even though his brothers meant it for evil, God meant it for good.
- When **Gideon** and his three hundred followers with their broken pitchers and lamps put the Midianites to flight, they were in the minority, but the battle was won and God was honored.

- When **Elijah** prayed down fire from heaven and put the prophets of Baal to shame, he was in the minority, but he won the day.
- When **David,** ridiculed by his brothers, went out to meet the giant Goliath, in size and influence young David was in a decided minority, but God ruled that day, and the enemy was defeated.
- When **Jesus** was crucified by Roman soldiers, by all appearances He seemed to be in a conspicuous minority, but He didn't stay on the cross, nor did He remain in the tomb. He arose, and He lives today for you, for me, and for a world waiting to have a reason to face the future with boldness and courage. With God as the source of our power, we will never be in the minority, and we will never be alone.

Do we have our hearts set on God? Do we want to elevate our relationships with our Creator to new levels? Have we had enough of business-as-usual religion, playing church, attending meetings that are meaningless, and seeing no real influence in our witness on the lives of others? If you are compelled to say yes, then I hope you are persuaded to be attentive to the call of God for your life. He may have been calling you all the time, but the noise of life and the distractions of daily living may have kept that call from falling on your ears. This may be the moment you say with Job, "Teach me, and I will be quiet; show me where I have been wrong" (Job 6:24 NIV). Or to pray with the psalmist, "Be still before the LORD and wait patiently for him" (Ps. 37:7 NIV).

It's only in silence and humble prayer that we will ever know God's best for our lives. It's my earnest prayer that you will have the courage to step into His presence as your first step to facing the future boldly with your loving, Almighty God. If that is your decision, please enter into His powerful presence through prayer and fasting. As we humble ourselves *individually* to pray and fast, an awakening will also come to our churches, our nation, and our world, but it will only come to others when it first comes to you. The secret to greatness is to humble ourselves before God in days or seasons of prayer and fasting, God's gateway to spiritual breakthroughs.

A PERSONAL DISCOVERY

It took at least two forty-day fasts for me to discover that I had only four problems in my life:

Problem 1: My mind.

Problem 2: My will.

Problem 3: My emotions.

Problem 4: My body.

I have a mind that wants to think about all kinds of things, and I have a real struggle with where it wants to go at times. My will is strong and, at times in opposition to the will of God. I have a set of emotions that are up and down, almost uncontrollable sometimes. I inhabit a body that is decaying regardless of how much I attempt to train it.

You have the same problems. Are you relieved to discover you only have four problems?

I believe that Scripture teaches you are body, soul, and spirit. This is what you are comprised of according to 1 Thessalonians 5:23. God is in the process of sanctifying us, setting us apart toward holiness.

Since we are comprised of body, soul, and spirit, then let me tell you what I believe. I believe if you know Jesus personally, He lives within your spirit. Your spirit with the Spirit of Jesus is always right with God, always in oneness, always in complete fellowship. I believe the soul is comprised of the mind, the will, and the emotions. Yes, the soul is comprised of three of your biggest problems. Then the body, oh the body. You know, that which we associate as being someone or the way they look, but in reality the body only serves as the tent in which we live.

We have a hard time seeing Jesus living through us or others at times because of what I just described. The spirit, which is in complete oneness with Jesus, always right with Him, has a hard time ever getting to the surface. In order to live through us or shine through us, the spirit has to get through the challenges of the mind, the will, the emotions, and the body.

The Holy Spirit serves like an orchestra conductor. When a conductor raises his hands to conduct a symphony, all raise their instruments. While individually they may sound weak or strange, as they follow the conductor together, they make a beautiful symphony of music we enjoy. Remember, the conductor calls them to order and conducts them together.

The Holy Spirit in your spirit is the conductor. When you pray and fast, your spirit, which has struggled to come to the surface, all of a sudden begins to stand in attention and alertness to the Holy Spirit of God. As the prayer and fasting journey matures, God's Spirit so stands up in your spirit that all of a sudden your spirit within, empowered by the Holy Spirit, begins to call the mind, will, emotions, and body into order. "Mind, get in order and get focused." "Will, submit to the will of God!" "Emotions, follow suit and come into the heart of God and feel what He feels." "Body, submit to the Lord right now."

This spiritual phenomenon happens when you pray and fast. Your life "gets it together" even in the midst of enormous challenges. ALL of you (mind, will, emotions, and body) become subject to the Spirit's leadership, who has made your spirit more alive than ever before. Again, prayer and fasting not only call these into order but awake your spirit. God does the work, but your submitting to Him in prayer and fasting sanctifies you to be like Jesus.

When this dynamic happens, you can face the future boldly with God. Even greater, you can rise up with your church to pursue God. And that's where you will enter a new dimension, one greater than you can imagine. Read on.

REFLECTION QUESTIONS

1. Are you fearful of the future or facing your future boldly?

2. What has God put in your heart about your future?

3. How valuable is prayer and fasting in your discovering your future?

In the local church at Antioch . . . as they were ministering to the Lord and fasting, the Holy Spirit said, "Set apart for Me Barnabas and Saul for the work that I have called them to." Then after they had fasted, prayed, and laid hands on them, they sent them off. Being sent by the Holy Spirit, they . . .
—Acts 13:1–4

I proclaimed a fast. . . . So we fasted and pleaded with our God about this, and He granted our request.
—Ezra 8:21, 23

Chapter Seven

Rising Up with Your Church to Pursue God

For too long the world has seen what the church can do. *It is time, past time, for the world to see what God can do.* Through the gateway of prayer and fasting, the church will rise up and have the life of God expressed through it.

When Christ followers embrace the principle of prayer and fasting into their lives, we know they will come away with this conviction: *God can do more in a moment than I could ever do in a lifetime.*

Can you imagine what the spiritual potential would be in your church if it embraced the principle of prayer and fasting? Can you imagine what would happen if your pastor became convicted of this need not only personally but also in leading his church? Can you imagine, pastor, what would happen, if your people began personally and corporately with you entering into moments of prayer and fasting?

Can I tell you what would happen? You will walk away with this conviction: *God can do more in moment than I could ever do in a lifetime.* God can also do more in and through the church in a moment than programs, ministries, technical excellence, great worship, or mere machinery. No one can take the place of God. Nothing can take the place of God.

I am weary of what I hear about the passivity of churches today in our nation and world. While many churches sleep or act daily as if they are out for an evening drive, many other churches are chasing the latest fad for the church today.

It appears that most are looking for short-term success and a shortcut to get there. What is the problem?

When we look at the church today, we are seeing what man can do. While we may have greater technology or more expressive worship or more fine-tuned targeted ministries, let me ask you this: *Do we have more of God?* I am convinced today more than ever before in my ministry that it past time for the church to see what God can do.

A lost, dying, desperate world needs to see what an alive, biblically based, God-empowered, Great Commission-driven church can do! I want to assure you, prayer and fasting can help your church become those things. Prayer and fasting move the focus off what we can do and adjust the focus to what God can do.

I am overflowing with urgency in calling the church to rise up and pursue God together through prayer and fasting. If we prayed for souls to come to Christ half as much as we prayed for people to get healed, we would have a whole lot more people saved and even a whole lot more people healed. Just imagine, your church, my church, the church of America, coming together to pray and fast for our nation to come to Christ.

The time is not tomorrow. The time is not later. The time is now. We are living in critical times, and critical times call for radical, urgent actions to occur. Urgent actions we can do personally and in our church include prayer and fasting.

In this chapter I am going to talk to you about how your church can rise up together to embrace the principle of prayer and fasting. If your church rises up together in prayer and fasting, the world will see what God can do.

How Can the Church Rise Up to Pray and Fast?

I have gone back into the archives of my ministry here in Northwest Arkansas. As I have researched how we have risen up together as a church into moments or seasons of prayer and fasting, I was both encouraged and disappointed. I was encouraged we had done it so many times. At the same time I was disappointed I had not led our people more when I began to recount all the things God did when we prayed and fasted as a church.

I want to give you several ideas of what you could do to rise up with your church to pray and fast. Remember, fasting is abstinence from food with a spiritual goal in mind, a time when you neglect the most natural thing your body desires in order to pursue the God of heaven to do something supernatural in your life. With this revisited briefly, what are some ways you could rise up with your church in prayer and fasting?

One-Meal Fast

A one-meal fast with your church is a good place to begin. In fact, you may begin even more simply with calling the church to fast over a specific meal, like lunch or dinner.

I am not going to assume anything. Please remember, they must know what they are fasting for when they retreat to prayer during that mealtime.

I have called our people to pray and fast over a Sunday noon meal for a solemn assembly we were having on a Sunday night. I challenged them to abstain from the Sunday lunchtime, go to a private place, and deal with God about their life in preparation for the solemn assembly that night. A solemn assembly is the gathering of the church for the purpose of repentance and crying out to God for revival.

How specific should you get? Let me quote directly from an article I wrote many years ago in our weekly church periodical:

The Sunday noon meal on January 9 is also the time we are setting aside to fast. Then *after the solemn assembly*, the fast can be broken. The solemn assembly has been called for the purpose of crying out to the Lord for spiritual renewal personally, in our church, and in America. As we come together for the purpose of renewing fellowship with God, we will experience repentance, cleansing, and renewal. Pray with me this week about this solemn assembly. This will be new ground for some of us, but the foundation is solid since it is based on the Bible. I believe God is going to meet with us mightily in the assembly.

I believe God's people will move toward this kind of initial commitment to prayer and fasting when they understand it. Biblical and practical teaching on fasting is important to do, but also specificity is imperative for success to occur.

Always be challenged to take the specified mealtime to draw aside privately and talk to God as well as listen to what He is saying to you from the Word.

Obviously, while we have done this for a solemn assembly, it could be done for anything. A one-meal fast is a good place to begin.

One-Day Fast

I believe the church will respond well when a pastor calls his people to a one-day fasting journey. I have done this numerous times through the years, too many to recount. It is simple enough that most can get their arms around it and their hearts into it.

We have called people to one-day fasting journeys for a specific need in our church all the way to the needs of our nation. At times we have encouraged people to fast for the National Day of Prayer, which is always the first Thursday in May.

In relating it to our church specifically, I have led our people to do a one-day fast to seek the Lord for specific major events in our church, from a day of emphasis we may be having, to a scheduled weeklong event that needs to be saturated with a deep commitment to prayer. We have also observed one-day fasts for the financial needs of our church to just asking God for a fresh touch of His Spirit in our church.

You can think of numerous events or desires for your life, church, nation, or world in which we could pray and fast. I do believe as your pastor and church leaders pray about having a one-day period of prayer and fasting for something, an important question may help guide them: *What is God wanting to do among us?* This can relate to a spiritual movement desired or needed. It can also relate to an upcoming event on the calendar.

When I lead our people into a one-day time of prayer and fasting, I encourage them not to eat from sundown until sundown. In other words, begin the fast at sundown on one day and conclude the fast at sundown the day after. I believe this is a proven and right model.

Seven-Day Corporate Fast

In both 2002 and 2007, I led our people to participate in a seven-day corporate fast. I had never done anything like that before but just felt led strongly to lead our people to go above and beyond. Our church had journeyed into several types of fasts, but this time I believed God wanted to take us into a new dimension not only as a church but for many of our people personally.

As I prayed about it, I asked God for specific direction. As always, in God's timing I received that direction. Both experiences were powerful, and for most who participated, life changing.

Our first seven-day corporate fast was special. I stood up on a Sunday morning a few weeks before, preaching on prayer and fasting. At that time I began to cast the vision to them. I believed God wanted us to pray and fast for seven days for two things. I challenged them to discover their greatest personal life burden and fast for that to be removed. At the same time, in the same fast, I wanted them to join me in praying and fasting for our church's greatest burden. Therefore, we were going to pray and fast for seven days for their greatest personal burden and our church's greatest burden.

I challenged them to go with us on this journey to the level they sensed God wanted them to do so but also the level they sensed they could do so physically. The latter was communicated because some people can only do so much due to medication they are on or various physical limitations that may exist. I wanted their participation. You see, while food is the usual thing abstained from in fasting, it could also be something that an individual loves almost as much as food.

So for four weeks, including the week I preached the initial sermon with this vision, we asked people to sign up on a commitment card their level of fasting on this journey with us.

I called them during the time of public invitation to come down, lay the card on the altar, asking God for the strength to do it.

Additionally, I wrote a seven-day corporate prayer guide we distributed to these people, but also to the entire church. I wanted our people to at least pray or know what we were doing. The guide was several pages long and would lead them through this time.

We also opened worship centers on both of our campuses for prayer throughout the day, but also had prayer and share services nightly. These were led by one of our pastors, where they read Scripture, led in organized prayer gatherings, concluding with leading a share time of what God is doing in them and through them. These prayer and share gatherings were one hour in length. I did not pressure our people to come, but told them to come as they felt they needed the encouragement. Personally, I only went to a couple of them that week.

God moved greatly. We had people from senior adults to children participate at some level. This kind of commitment was so new that we only received from 855 people complete commitment cards. Of these cards 304 people did a complete seven-day fast with us, drinking only water or juice. Another fifty-six people fasted from their favorite meal of the day. Another ninety-eight people ate only one meal a day. Another sixty-nine people did the Daniel fast, eating only vegetables. Another twenty-three only prayed due to health restrictions, and obviously many others who only prayed did not feel compelled to sign up to do so. Another thirty-three people went on an Internet and television fast, meaning no Internet or television for those seven days. Another thirteen people wrote in creative ways they were going to participate. Finally, 259 of our children participated in all kinds of varied ways.

How did I feel about receiving only 855 commitment cards from our people, knowing we touch several thousand people a week? I rejoiced greatly. Having 855 people on some kind of journey with me, of which 304 were praying and fasting for all seven days was unprecedented. Few pastors I know have ever even done a seven-day fast, and we had 304 people participate in doing one. I was thrilled. Sure, others could have done it, but listen, this is big-time stuff. This was a strong commitment requested, not some shallow experience with a low commitment level.

Five years later we believed God was leading us to another seven-day corporate fast. This time we called it "Breakthrough 2007." We challenged the church to pray and fast for this period of time for a personal breakthrough and a church breakthrough.

Let me ask you, what is the wall or situation or obstacle you need to come down in your life? Identify it and then join me in prayer and fasting for it. Our church need was for a breakthrough for our future. This was our greatest need.

More specifically for our church, I led us to see we needed breakthroughs spiritually: we needed a spiritual downpour; breakthroughs strategically: we needed a defined direction; and breakthroughs financially: we needed financial miracles.

As I had done before, I wrote a specific prayer guide, called them to make commitments to go with us on this journey, plus we had the prayer and share gatherings nightly, and as before, God moved greatly. On this second seven-day corporate fast, 1,387 people participated with us at some level. I will not go into the specifics of how they participated as I did before, but we went from 855 to 1,387 commitment cards being completed.

Both journeys were powerful, meaningful, challenging, but also life changing for so many of our people. As they entered this kind of territory, they had to experience a new level of God strengthening and guiding them.

I share this with you to give you ideas, never to boast or bring attention to our church or myself. These things were all for Jesus, no one else.

Pray about your church going on a seven-day corporate fast together. Whether you have fifty people, five hundred people, fifteen hundred people, or multiple thousands attending your church, whoever God wants to go on the journey with you will go, and they will never be the same because of it. People respond to leadership. Lead them to deepen their walk with God through prayer and fasting. It is God's gateway to spiritual breakthroughs. There is nothing like rising up with your church to pursue God.

Forty-Day Corporate Fast

On several occasions in our history, we have led the church to be a part of a forty-day fasting journey. No, I am not talking about individuals doing forty days by themselves, but the church going for forty days. The individual would be challenged to fast one day during that forty days or however many days they desired during that period of time.

Our church has done forty-day corporate fasting for evangelistic events. In 1993 we did this for a major evangelistic event. We were praying and fasting for one thousand people to come to Christ over a seven-day period of time. On the first night after the event, we had a driving snowstorm that gave our region several inches of snow, resulting in school being dismissed for several days. On the surface this was not good, but we added two more gatherings on that Monday, all in faith due to our fasting and prayer.

Miraculously, after day seven was completed, in that one week we witnessed more than twenty-six hundred people come to saving faith in Jesus Christ. All for Jesus! God heard our cry in prayer and fasting and did what only God could do. It was incredible!

We have done forty-day corporate fasting for revival, and on another occasion we have done a forty-day corporate fasting journey for a mighty outpouring of the Holy Spirit to be upon our church. Our hope and prayer was for God to move among us powerfully. Additionally, our heart has always been for America so this was also in relationship to our nation as well. Prayer and fasting really give me the heartbeat that God is going to bring a mighty revival to America that will cross over all cultural, racial, ethnic, and denominational lines. Before Jesus returns, I believe we will see it occur.

We have done forty-day corporate fasting with our denomination for revival. Earlier in the preface I shared about the experience in 1996. As part of that personal prayer and fasting experience, leading up to that preaching opportunity, God gave me a strategic plan for the fall that year. That plan was not only for my church but also for the churches in our denomination. The strategy I believe God gave me included:

- On the last Sunday morning of October, pastors would preach on fasting and prayer.
- On that Sunday night pastors would lead their church in a solemn assembly.
- On the last Wednesday in October, all churches would participate in a day of humiliation, prayer, and fasting for the spiritual goal of seeing personal, church, and national revival.
- The following Sunday, pastors would center their

preaching on personal, church, and national revival, challenging God's people to whatever it takes to see revival in America.

These things originated with what God put in my heart to preach at that 1996 gathering in the annual convention sermon.

Thousands of churches within our own denomination participated as well as countless thousands of Christ followers. Additionally, many churches and denominational groups participated way beyond Southern Baptist churches. This took place because of the amazing momentum God gave to the vision initially, then through opportunities where God opened doors for me to share on *Focus on the Family, The 700 Club*, and many others.

We have also done forty-day corporate fasting in relationship to a major financial campaign. We did this in our most recent major campaign called "Special Treasures." Our people chose their day or days and moved forward with great eagerness and faith to pray and fast. The end result was the largest financial campaign in our history, resulting in it being four times what we have ever done before in a three-year window. We did not use a consultant, but we prayed. I cast the vision in at least forty different settings for our adults, and God blessed powerfully. We saw God's people commit more than twenty-five million dollars to Special Treasures.

One of the great stories of that campaign was about a wedding ring a woman gave to me in our first gathering. It was literally all she had to give. It was the most humbling experience in giving I had ever experienced as she laid it in my hand, weeping. After continuing to cast the vision to our people, I felt led one night to tell the story and ask: "Will someone buy this ring, and when you do, will you give it back? It is God's ring." God kept one of our men up all night, and early that next morning he wanted to buy it for five thousand dollars. The next night I stood up to a different group, told the story, and asked them, "Is there anyone who wants to buy the ring for ten thousand dollars and when you do, will you give it back? It is God's ring." Before I left that night, a couple bought the ring.

I did the same the next night, and someone bought it for twenty thousand dollars. I kept on doing it, and we had it going for forty thousand dollars, then eighty thousand dollars, and yes, then one hundred sixty thousand dollars. Finally, a man called me and bought it for a huge amount, resulting in the ring giving that campaign more than $1.3 million. All of this due to a simple sacrificial gift of a ring with not much value by the world at all. Oh how God used it! He is amazing!

I am convinced that it was the journey of prayer and fasting for forty days that resulted in such radical giving. Only God, yes, only God could have done all of that. When you pray and fast, God can do more in a moment than you could ever do in a lifetime.

In all of these various experiences I have just shared with you, each one of those journeys went by a prayer plan for all forty days. As I wrote each of those plans, the Lord directed

His people to honor Him through prayer and fasting. Obviously, God answers prayer.

THE VALUE OF A PRAYER AND FASTING GUIDE

I really believe a guide for people in corporate prayer and fasting is imperative. While it could be done another way, it just does not make sense for all to be doing their own thing. Without a doubt God always customizes the journey for all of us. He works uniquely in all of us.

I believe there are four major reasons a prayer and fasting guide is important when you are leading your church in a prayer and fasting journey.

Spiritual Goal

Fasting is abstinence from food with a spiritual goal in mind. The prayer guide defines the goal specifically and leads everyone to pray toward that goal. The only way to stay focused is to have the spiritual goal articulated in a plan. Every request in the plan turns people to praying for the same spiritual goal.

Oneness

Another major reason a prayer and fasting guide is important is because it helps create a sense of unity. It promotes unity of spirit and oneness of heart. There is something unusually dynamic when we focus on the same thing together.

Oneness is important and essential according to John 17. We need to learn the value and dynamic of oneness in prayer and fasting. Just knowing someone else, or twenty people, or five hundred people are praying at the same time for the same thing can elevate the entire church.

Specific

Powerful praying occurs when you pray specifically.

Can you imagine your entire church praying for the same spiritual goal in complete oneness with one another and even with specificity over each request? Powerful! Life changing! God-sized results! This is why the prayer guides I design are prayed over by me first and designed with specificity.

Consistency

When you have a spiritual goal before you, knowing others are praying with you over the same specific prayer guide, then you will be consistent in the journey. I believe we organize most things, but at times we do not organize prayer. The Holy Spirit can lead you in the plan as much as during the process. If He wants to change the plan in the middle of the process, so be it. Consistency is important in corporate prayer journeys and is usually accomplished when all of these are a part of the journey.

RISING UP

I am not sure anything is more powerful than the church rising up to pursue God through the disciplines of prayer and fasting. While the walls around us seem too high, too deep, and too thick to overcome, through prayer and fasting each wall can be crushed and destroyed. When the church comes together in prayer and fasting, a mighty army is rising up to ascend the hills toward God, and NOTHING can stand in its way. Yes, for too long the world has seen what the church can do. Now is the time for the world to see what God can do through the church! How does this happen? It happens when we rise up by falling down as a church to pray and fast!

When we do, we will see it is supernaturally powerful. This will confirm again: prayer and fasting *are* God's gateway to spiritual breakthroughs. Prayer and fasting will lead you to seeing your church experience God.

 ## REFLECTION QUESTIONS

1. Has your church ever set aside a time to pray and fast together? If not, why?

2. If your church was called to a fast, would you participate?

3. What do you see as the greatest need in your church? Would you be willing to fast for it?

Call to Me and I will answer you and tell you great and wondrous things you do not know.
—Jeremiah 33:3

For nothing will be impossible with God.
—Luke 1:37

Now to Him who is able to do above and beyond all that we ask or think—according to the power that works in you—to Him be glory in the church and in Christ Jesus to all generations, forever and ever. Amen.
—Ephesians 3:20–21

Chapter Eight

Seeing Your Church Experience God

One day a young lumberjack challenged an older coworker to a contest. Both wanted to see which man could fell the most trees in a single day. By sundown it was obvious the older lumberjack had won hands down. The younger fellow couldn't figure it out. He had chopped nonstop all day while the older lumberjack had stopped every hour. When asked how he had won the contest, the older man explained, "Every time I sat down, I sharpened my ax."

Just as we can't cut down trees with dull axes, we will never be the men and women God created us to be if our spirits are not honed to razor-edged sharpness. I do not know of anything more capable of sharpening your life spiritually than prayer and fasting. I do not know of anything your church can do to become more focused and effective than prayer and fasting. For the Christ follower who wants to go on with God in a greater way, *I believe prayer and fasting will accelerate your growth exponentially.*

An example of this is my dear friend and ministry partner, John Cope. For almost eight years John served as our student pastor. He was committed to the things of God then and has grown in his walk with God exponentially. Why? Let me tell you the story.

In 2001 John and his family moved to Philadelphia, Pennsylvania, to start the Keystone Community Church. It was a challenging task, and many days were filled with immense disappointment. However, God began to use the situation to work in John's life greatly, moving him into seasons of prayer and fasting. The results are absolutely amazing. He sent me this a few days ago.

Please read this testimony:

> The practical insights from your original book, *The Power of Prayer and Fasting,* and being able to shadow you for nearly eight years allowed me to gain much wisdom as it relates to prayer and fasting. I have

learned as a leader my greatest edge is to hear from heaven.

Prayer and fasting put me in a great position to come into agreement with God's agenda. Since starting Keystone Church, we have experienced several corporate fasts; our longest one has been thirty days. I personally have completed several extended fasts; my longest was thirty-seven days. Our staff goes prayer walking before our staff meetings. I've seen God start a church from a team of *five people* who, when moved to Philadelphia in 2001, knew absolutely no one. We have now planted four churches. Keystone Community Fellowship presently averages eleven hundred people in attendance. Our first capital campaign raised $3.1 million dollars. God has blessed us with two separate properties, one of four acres and another of forty-one acres. We had a couple move up from First Baptist of Woodstock, Georgia. They became discouraged with the lack of the gospel in their neighborhood. They lived thirty minutes from Keystone, and we prayed for their area on many occasions. They eventually were transferred back to the south. When they moved, we had zero people attending our church from their area. Presently we have over one hundred people that live in that area. This fall we will begin a multisite in their community. Another example of prayer and fasting, besides the above, is we had an eighty-year-old

Jewish woman give her heart to Christ. Thanks, Ronnie. I appreciate your support.

John's testimony fires me up! John Cope is seeing his church experience God. It does not matter whether your church is in rural America, county seat America, urban America, or inner-city America. It does not matter if it is declining in membership, plateaued in attendance, or growing rapidly. What matters is that each pastor and church gets their edge from heaven! Prayer and fasting are the gateway to giving you that heavenly edge that leads to major spiritual breakthroughs.

What can John's church have in common with your church? Well, if your church has a major movement of God due to humbling yourselves in prayer and fasting, you can have commonality with him. The people may be different. The names will not be the same. The style may even be 180 degrees different. None of that matters. What matters most is that your church sees and experiences God mightily. Pastor John and Keystone Fellowship of Philadelphia are paying the price and the results are God honoring and God sized. They are results that are all for Jesus.

NINE WAYS YOUR CHURCH WILL EXPERIENCE GOD WHEN YOU PRAY AND FAST

It is often assumed by some that prayer and fasting have just become a new thing in my life and in my church. Earlier in the book I told you about when I started praying and fasting in college. All these years it has been a part of my life as I have sensed God's leadership to pray and fast.

It is not something new for me in leading a church to pray and fast corporately. As I went back into the archives, I was reminded of an incredible story of seeing my church experience God.

From 1981 to 1983, I had one of the greatest privileges of my life serving as the pastor of the First Baptist Church of Palacios, Texas. Palacios is a coastal town located on the Gulf of Mexico between Houston and Corpus Christi.

When I became pastor, the church was touching about one hundred and twenty people a week; and when I was called away three years later, we were touching just under four hundred people weekly. It was a special place that Jeana and I love to this day.

Some of this miraculous movement in that town of just over four thousand people occurred due to our church praying and fasting. In early 1983 we were preparing for a city-wide tent crusade. The tent being put up in downtown drew major attention. This is what I said to the church in March 1983:

> I am asking you to pray and fast as a church from Tuesday evening, March 12, beginning at 5:30 p.m., until Wednesday evening, March 13, at 5:30 p.m. The fast will be for twenty-four hours! It will be culminated in a prayer rally here at the church at 7:30 p.m. on Wednesday evening. The purpose will be

to petition God for one hundred souls to be saved in this crusade! Every time you are supposed to eat, get alone for thirty minutes and pray. When you get hungry, read your Bible and pray and ask God to control your appetites. It will be basically a food fast! Drink water, coffee, tea, or juices. That is all! Twenty-four hours for God and the souls of Palacios! Be quiet about the fast. Do not complain about it.

What did we see happen? We saw more than one hundred people come to know Jesus Christ as Lord and Savior in that tent crusade. I am convinced God heard our pleas as we prayed and fasted.

God moved miraculously in that three-year stretch due to moments like this that were spent in prayer and fasting.

Whether in Palacios, Texas, or our church in Northwest Arkansas, or hearing stories from other churches that practice prayer and fasting, we know that we see the church experience God when prayer and fasting is practiced. What I have seen God do is amazing. His movement is inexplicable and unexplainable! God responds powerfully when He sees His church pursue Him in prayer and fasting.

Below are the nine ways your church will experience God when they pray and fast:

Focus

When your church prays and fasts together, a great focus occurs. No longer is the spiritual lens blurred or smeared. God begins to orchestrate an amazing focus not only in your life but also in your church. This focus happens as the Holy Spirit calls the spirit of your church to order!

Just as the lumberjack took the time to sit down and focus on sharpening the ax, the church has to slow down at times and be sharpened through the spiritual crucible of prayer and fasting. Churches are just like people. They get busy, operate in extreme distractedness, and lose their effectiveness. Prayer and fasting call the church to focus.

Wonder

As the church prays and fasts, you become aware of the wonder of God! As you focus spiritually, you discover God is who He says He is, and He can do what He says He can do. No longer do you sing songs of the faith, and they mean nothing. You get caught up in the wonder of who God is!

Prayer and fasting really make you aware of the Lord and His wondrous works. You no longer can just move through life with a casual view of God. If we are not careful, we will be so casual in life that we are casual in dealing with God. God is *not* your buddy, but He is God. Prayer and fasting make you aware of God's holiness and open your eyes to His great wonder.

Sensitivity

When your church prays and fasts together, an unusual sensitivity occurs. Your church will become sensitive to God and the leadership of His Spirit. Can you imagine your church being led by the Holy Spirit of God and you responding accordingly, even if it is not in the bulletin or planned on the program for the day? Prayer and fasting make the church sensitive to the Holy Spirit of God.

This sensitivity does not stop here but is sensed, and even felt, in the fellowship as a whole. Christians become sensitive to other Christians. This sensitivity flows through the fellowship as compassion toward others becomes important. As your church prays and fasts together, sensitivity will occur.

Unity

When the church prays and fasts together, unity will occur. Those who cannot or do not choose to participate in a fasting journey with you will still sense the unifying effect of prayer and fasting.

Churches all over our land are so disrupted with division. Church bullies are tearing up many of our churches as they exert their carnal power. Division within the church, whether it is over territorialism and power or lack of leadership by the pastor or worship styles or anything else, is all driven by demonic influences and is from hell. I realize for some of you that may be a little strong, but let's get it straight. *If your church is not living in unity, your church needs to get right with God.* The Holy Spirit brings unity to the body.

This is why your church needs to pray and fast. It has a unifying influence and result in the church. Jesus is always pleased when His church is one with one another. Prayer and fasting can provide the needed spiritual breakthrough that will move you toward unity.

Growth

A prayer and fasting journey in your church will bring growth to those who participate. Most Christians don't feel challenged to do something radical like pray and fast for a season. Therefore, when they respond positively, the result is growth.

They develop a healthy and spiritual attitude, "God led me to do this, and by His grace and only through His power, I did it." This results in what I call a "therefore spirit," meaning, therefore, whatever it is God wants me to do, I can do it with His grace and by His power. We call this growth!

Prayer and fasting grow Christians and grow churches. Churches grow spiritually and at times even numerically. Prayer and fasting result in growth.

Anticipation

When the church prays and fasts together, there is a holy anticipation that is electric. People look forward to seeing what God is going to do. They anticipate Him working powerfully. *Dread* is no longer a word used in connection with attending church. *Anticipation* is in, and *dread* is out.

When people have experienced God personally during the week, they are anticipating what God is going to do on Sunday. Due to their spiritual sensitivity increasing, they excitedly anticipate what God is going to do in their church. If your church has lost its anticipation, pray and fast.

Enlargement

An enlargement of a church's vision occurs when the church is involved in praying and fasting. No longer do we talk about whether we cannot and should not do something, but we talk about how we are going to do it.

So many churches have lost their vision. Clarity in vision is also missing. When your church prays and fasts together, vision will begin to be clarified. As He reveals His desire for your church, you will begin to see it from His perspective, and you will enter into an enlargement of your vision.

Engagement

When the church prays and fasts together, we begin to engage the community around us like never before. We begin to see needs for the first time, even though they have existed for a long time. As a church engages its community, we will feel the pain, illness, hurt, disappointment, discouragement, but also the joy. All of these exist within a community.

Prayer and fasting result in your church engaging those around you. You can no longer live like a hermit or stick your head in the sand. The needs of your community are screaming for your attention, and for the first time you are not only hearing them, but you are going to answer their screams.

Advancement

As the church practices prayer and fasting, we advance toward fulfilling the Great Commission more than ever before. We have a desire to see people come to Christ, be baptized, and discipled in their faith. We see the need to do this regionally, nationally, and globally.

As our church has prayed and fasted through the years, doors have opened all over our region, nation, and world. Our church is committed not only to a multisite ministry but also to planting many churches. This year alone, we are investing in and launching fourteen churches around the world. Some of these will be local, others national, and most will be international.

In the last eight years since our church launched our Pinnacle Hills campus, where a multi-thousand attend church weekly, we have also invested in and planted thirty-four churches around our region, America, and the world. I believe prayer and fasting have been used by God to advance this movement globally.

Advancement toward fulfilling the Great Commission is my heart. Through prayer and fasting God clarified our missional vision as a church from Acts 1:8 more than a decade ago: *Reaching Northwest Arkansas, America, and the World for Jesus Christ*. My heart is on fire to share with the world the saving grace of Jesus Christ. We cannot sit still or be idle; we must advance the gospel into the entire world. The world needs the gospel of Jesus Christ. Prayer and fasting advance the church in its goal to fulfill the Great Commission.

People are lost without Jesus. People need Jesus. Prayer and fasting propels the church forward in its advancement toward fulfilling the Great Commission of Jesus Christ.

GOD WILL CREATE A STORY IN YOU

When you and your church practice prayer and fasting, *God will create a story in you.* Your story will not be like John Cope's or like mine. God will customize His work in you, resulting in your story being customized by God Himself.

Yes, prayer and fasting will become a powerful, spiritual dynamite for you and your church. Regardless of what stands in your way or your church's way to being all you need to be, rest assured and be convinced today: Prayer and fasting *is* God's gateway to spiritual breakthroughs.

The players in your story will not be the same as mine. The situations or circumstances may even be radically different.

Yet God will be the same! While the stories will be different, you will come away believing with all your heart as I do: *God can do more in a moment than I could ever do in a lifetime.*

REFLECTION QUESTIONS

1. Would you like to see your church experience God together on a fasting journey?

2. Out of the nine ways a church can experience God in their fasting journey, which two or three ways does your church need to experience God?

3. Will you talk to your pastor or to your church about a corporate fast, sharing with them the vision of this book?

Our Daily Prayer Guide

"If we confess our sins, He is faithful and righteous to forgive us our sins and to cleanse us from all unrighteousness."
—1 John 1:9

INVENTORY OF THE HEART

Review this once each day, especially during the first three days of the fast. Please go through the guide carefully. Personalize the prayers for your church and region.

The following is taken from an earlier chapter.

I have kept the verses and their poignant, embarrassing questions close at hand during my fasts as a reminder that, if I was going to be serious about knowing God's holiness, I would need to look at an entire landscape of issues. I share these with you with a heart that invites you to be quite honest with yourself and honest with God as you reflect on your answers. This is an important exercise because when you and I choose to enter the gateway to God's supernatural power and live in the presence of His holiness, we must become persuaded that every "yes" to these questions suggests there is a sin for us to confess.

1. "In everything give thanks; for this is the will of God in Christ Jesus for you" (1 Thess. 5:18 NKJV).

Do I worry about anything? Have I forgotten to thank God for all things, the seemingly bad as well as the good? Do I neglect to give Him thanks for my breath, my health, and for life itself?

2. "Now to Him who is able to do exceedingly abundantly above all that we ask or think, according to the power that works in us" (Eph. 3:20 NKJV).

Do I shy away from attempting to do things in the name of my heavenly Father because I fear I am not talented enough? Do feelings of inferiority keep me from serving God? When I do accomplish something of merit, do I choose to give myself, rather than God, the glory?

3. "You shall receive power when the Holy Spirit has come upon you; and you shall be witnesses to Me in Jerusalem, and in all Judea and Samaria, and to the end of the earth" (Acts 1:8 NKJV).

Have I believed it's good enough to live my Christianity in a casual manner and that it's not all that important to share the good news of my deliverance with others?

4. "I say . . . to everyone who is among you, not to think of himself more highly than he ought to think" (Rom. 12:3 NKJV).

Am I overly proud of my accomplishments, my talents, my family? Do I have difficulty putting the concerns of others first? Do I have a rebellious spirit at the thought that God may want to change me and rearrange my thinking?

5. **"Let all bitterness, wrath, anger, clamor, and evil speaking be put away from you, with all malice" (Eph. 4:31 NKJV).**

Do I complain, find fault, argue? Do I nurse and delight in a critical spirit? Do I carry a grudge against believers of another group, denomination, or theological persuasion because they don't see the truth as I see it? Do I speak unkindly about people when they are not present? Do I find that I'm often angry with myself? With others? With God?

6. **"Do you not know that your body is the temple of the Holy Spirit who is in you, whom you have from God, and you are not your own?" (1 Cor. 6:19 NKJV).**

Am I honoring God with my lifestyle and body?

7. **"Let no corrupt word proceed out of your mouth" (Eph. 4:29 NKJV).**

Do I use language that fails to edify others, tell off-color jokes or stories that demean another person's race, habits, or culture? Do I condone these comments when guests are in my home or when my colleagues share them with me at work?

8. **"Do not . . . give place to the devil" (Eph. 4:26–27 NKJV).**

Do I ignore the fact that I open myself to Satan when I participate in ungodly practices, psychic predictions, occult literature, and violent, sex-driven, sexually perverse movies and videos? Do I seek counsel for daily living from horoscopes in the paper, on television, or on the Internet rather than from God, my true and ultimate source for living? Do I let Satan use me to set up barriers that inhibit the cause of Christ in my church and home through criticism and gossip?

9. "Not slothful in business" (Rom. 12:11 KJV).

Am I chronically late in paying my debts, sometimes choosing not to pay them at all? Do I charge more on my credit cards than I can honestly afford to pay? Do I neglect to keep honest income tax records? Do I engage in shady business deals?

10. "Beloved, . . . abstain from fleshly lusts, which war against the soul" (1 Pet. 2:11 NKJV).

Am I guilty of a lustful eye toward the opposite sex? Do I fill my mind with sexually oriented TV programs, lewd movies, unsavory books and magazines? Their covers? Centerfolds? Especially when I sense no one is watching? Do I indulge in lustful activities that God's Word condemns, such as fornication, adultery, perversion?

11. "Bearing with one another, and forgiving one another, if anyone has a complaint against another; even as Christ forgave you, so you also must do" (Col. 3:13 NKJV).

Have I failed to forgive those who may have said or done something to hurt me? Have I written off certain people as not worthy of my friendship?

12. "Even so you also outwardly appear righteous to men, but inside you are full of hypocrisy and lawlessness." (Matt. 23:28 NKJV).

Do I know in my heart that I am often not what people see? Am I hiding behind being active in my church as a cover for my activities away from the body of Christ? Am I mimicking the Christian faith for social status, acceptance in my church or my community? Am I real?

13. "Finally, brethren, whatever things are true, whatever things are noble, whatever things are just, whatever things are pure, whatever things are lovely, whatever things are of good report, if there is any virtue and if there is anything praiseworthy—meditate on these things" (Phil. 4:8 NKJV).

Do I enjoy listening to conversation that hurts others? Do I pass it on? Do I believe rumors or partial truths, especially about an enemy or a competitor? Do I choose to spend little or no time each day allowing God to speak to me through His Word?

Your Personal Breakthrough

Use the previous Scriptures and questions to identify the areas in your life that need a breakthrough. Decide on one or two issues that you will seek God's will in this week.

You must organize this section yourself as you sense God leading you to pray. We have provided room to write down your plan as a part of the daily prayer guide.

After you finish praying and trusting God for your spiritual breakthrough, pray for everyone else in our fellowship who is fasting for their personal spiritual breakthrough. May the walls come down in each of our lives!

_____

_____

_____

_____

_____

_____

Our Church's Breakthrough
to the Future

Call to Me, and I will . . . show you great
and mighty things, which you do not know.
(Jer. 33:3 NKJV)

Again, I assure you: If two of you on earth agree about any matter that you pray for, it will be done for

you by My Father in heaven. For where two or three
are gathered together in My name,
I am there among them. (Matt. 18:19–20)

As we call to God together, praying in agreement, God
alone can show us great and mighty things we do not know,
even concerning the future for our church. Please join us in
lifting up our church in the following areas:

Confess the Sins of Our Church

Ask God to forgive us and to give us the power to repent
of our sins. Any of the following could be a sin in our per-
sonal lives and our church; each must be confessed and
turned away from, individually and as a church body.
Limited or missing:
- Excitement about Jesus Christ and what He is doing in
  our lives and church
- Enthusiasm for God and the things of God
- Focus on God and His work through our church
- Service to God through our church
- Love for people and the needs they have
- Involvement in ministry to others
- Attendance in worship services
- Involvement in a connection group
- Response privately or publicly when God's Word is
  preached or taught
- Desire for people to come to Christ
- Desire for our church to grow
- Passionate love for God

- Time or priority given to the things of God
- Love expressed for other Christ followers, resulting in a critical or judgmental spirit
- Submission to spiritual leaders
- Sensitivity to God's Word and His movement
- Honor and respect for God regarding the giving of the tithe (first tenth) and offerings to the local church
- Giving of "ALL God has given to you" by not tithing (giving one-tenth) of everything God has blessed you with from your gross salary to bonuses, land, stocks, bonds, inheritances, and your future wills and trusts when you die
- Burden to see Northwest Arkansas and your region reached for Jesus Christ and for God's people to see a mighty spiritual revival
- Desire to share our faith with family, friends, associates, or neighbors who desperately need Christ
- Desire to see people who are different from us come to Christ
- Desire to see the message of Jesus shared with Northwest Arkansas, America, and the world
- Desire to participate personally in God's work
- Desire for broken relationships to be restored
- Desire to engage and participate in private and public worship of God

Petition God for Our Church's Breakthrough to the Future

Ask God to grant each of the following requests as we seek His will and trust Him for our future:

SPIRITUALLY

- We need deliverance from the sins of our church.
- We need a spiritual downpour that will rain on us mightily.
- We need a drenching and anointing of God's Spirit.
- We need passion, enthusiasm, and fire for God, His activity, and our church.
- We need deeply spiritual men and women in our church body.
- We need God to call people into ministry and missions.
- We need God to do in us whatever is needed and do around us whatever is needed in order for us to be recipients of His special anointing, blessing, and calling as a church.
- We need a spiritual revival to occur on our campuses, in our worship services, and in our connection groups.
- We need a mighty, heaven-sent, Bible-based, Jesus-centered, Holy Spirit revival to happen in our churches, beginning in each of us today.
- We need God to break our hearts for friends, coworkers, neighbors, and family members who don't have a personal relationship with Jesus.

STRATEGICALLY

- We need a defined direction for our future.
- We need to dream without parameters about what God can and wants to do in our church.
- We need a defined strategy about how to reach a changing Northwest Arkansas and America.
- We need a defined strategy about how to reach the ethnic groups of our region.
- We need a defined strategy about how to do church in the twenty-first century.
- We need a defined strategy that is God sized.
- We need a defined strategy about what our church can do to reach Northwest Arkansas, America, and the world.
- We need a defined strategy for each age group in our church.
- We need a defined strategy about how to mobilize people for Christ in Northwest Arkansas but also around the world.
- We need a defined strategy about how to equip the ministers and missionaries God wants to connect us with in the future.
- We need God to give each of us a spirit of willingness to give up our preferences and to walk away from things that are hindering our ability to minister to as many people as possible in our region.
- We need the Lord to give us a clear vision for our future that we can articulate, run to, and lead our people to follow.

FINANCIALLY

- We need the walls of financial strongholds to be broken in our people.
- We need the national and local economy to move in a positive direction.
- We need our people to be blessed abundantly by God.
- We need our people to prosper financially with integrity in every way.
- We need major financial hurdles to be cleared in our church in order for us to seize the future wholeheartedly.
- We need our people to be obedient to God by giving generously at least one-tenth of all God has entrusted to them, including their wills and trust.
- We need God to clear any and all of the financial obstacles our church faces.
- We need God to bring and develop new givers in our church.
- We need God to meet our ministry budget for the coming year miraculously and generously.
- We need God to show our people how to create businesses that will generate funds for the cause of Christ.
- We need God's people to believe in the power and blessing of giving and to give generously and enthusiastically to the causes of Christ.
- We need God to provide our church with major financial miracles now that will impact our future dramatically.

Pray for This Week

Pray for God's power to be evident this week in the following areas:

- Pray for our nightly prayer services at 6:30 p.m. on each campus this week.
- Pray for our pastor and ministry staff team as they lead us this week.
- Pray for the following Sunday to be a powerful Spiritual Breakthrough Sunday for many individuals and our entire church.
- Pray that God will change our church forever spiritually, strategically, and financially.
- Pray that God will show you specific ways to change your life in order to bring Him more glory.

Thank God for Answered Prayer and Great Miracles for Yourself, Others, and Our Church

A Practical Guide:
Q & A with Ronnie Floyd

FASTING AND PRAYER AS
YOUR SPIRITUAL WORSHIP

The disciplines of prayer and fasting are not reduced to a formula or a hoop that we are to jump through as if we are in a kind of spiritual circus. Nor are they physical tests or exercises in mental discipline. True prayer and fasting are attitudes of the heart and cries of the soul. God's Word has a strong rebuke for those who fast for the wrong reasons or in an improper manner. I have never seen God respond favorably to prayer and/or fasting based on false pretenses or impure motives.

Improper Reasons/Motives

Prayer and fasting are improper when a person seeks . . .

- to fulfill selfish desires and ambitions.
- to attempt to manipulate God.
- to elevate one's status or personal agenda.
- to promote false piety, legalism, or religious duty.

Improper Manner

Prayer and fasting are improper when they . . .

- draw attention to personal glorification.
- are attempted without sufficient seriousness and respect.
- are conducted while intentionally continuing in sin.
- are conducted while continuing to pursue selfish desires in pleasure and business.
- are conducted while harboring improper, ungodly attitudes.
- are conducted while promoting or continuing injustice, oppression, or impropriety.
- are conducted without drawing aside daily and dedicating ample time for sincere seeking, quiet communion, and devoted prayer with God.

GOD-HONORING FAST

The Bible is filled with references to the prayers and fasting of His people. In Matthew 6, Jesus placed fasting on the same level as praying and giving. He said, "When you fast, when you pray, and when you give." I wonder why Christians today and churches in our generation don't place fasting on the same level as praying and giving? Jesus, by His example and His teaching, demonstrates that prayer and fasting are important and integral ingredients in the lives of His followers. One purpose of prayer and fasting is to bring our hearts to a place of being filled with a sacrificial love that results in godly attitudes in our lives. True fasting will draw us closer to God and His purposes.

I can't explain why God has chosen prayer and fasting as the gateway to supernatural power. One thing I do know: Scripture, prayer, and fasting are the ways believers humble themselves in the sight of the Lord. When we humble ourselves, He promises to exalt and lift us up at the appointed time (1 Pet. 5:6; James 4:10). God also indicates that He will resist the proud but will give grace to the humble (James 4:6). Again, 2 Chronicles 7:14 indicates the importance of humbling ourselves before God.

Fasting brings a sharp focus to the dramatic difference between our physical and spiritual natures. Eating is one of the most fundamental things we do as physical beings. One of the most natural desires is for food. Without proper nourishment we die. By exercising our wills and depriving ourselves of food for spiritual purposes, we acknowledge our spiritual natures and honor our Creator-Father. When we deny the natural for the purpose of calling upon God to do the supernatural, He will enable and empower us to experience the supernatural. Through fasting we confirm the words uttered by Jesus in the face of temptation during His forty-day fast, "Man does not live on bread alone, but on every word that comes from the mouth of God" (Matt. 4:4 NIV). Through prayer and fasting we forsake our own physical needs and the creature comforts of this world and call upon God as the Originator, Giver, Source, and Sustainer of all life, especially our own. We exalt Him as our hope and salvation. True spiritual fasting will result in submission and devotion to God.

God Blesses Us When Our Fasts . . .

- focus on Him and honor Him. (Although you will receive spiritual blessings, these are not proper motives for fasting.)
- have spiritual purposes. (Although you may realize certain physical benefits, these are not proper motives for spiritual fasting, e.g., for weight-loss purposes.)
- cause individuals to humble themselves and submit to the authority of God and His Word.
- cause individuals to acknowledge and repent of sin.
- deprive our natural desires and lusts to focus on the spiritual.

A PRACTICAL GUIDE

Even when we honor God by praying and fasting, this does not mean that our heavenly Father will grant everything on our wish-and-whim list. God will only work and bless in ways that are consistent and in harmony with His will and purpose. One of the primary functions of prayer and fasting is to help us discover what His ordained purposes and will are for our lives.

I have included some practical helps and hints that are rooted in my own experience—guidelines that I follow as I fast and pray.

Spiritual Suggestions

- If God does not call you to fast, don't fast! Most people don't have a call to fast possibly because they're not totally open to God's leadership, have not been taught the biblical foundation for fasting, or are caught up in other types of sin that interfere.
- Determine in advance the length of the fast God is calling you to undertake.
- If God calls you to a fast, He has specific reasons and purposes in mind. Before you fast, determine the purposes of your fast and write them down, e.g., Lord, I am fasting for the spiritual purposes of: (1) spiritual revival and awakening in the church of America, (2) spiritual revival and awakening in my own local church, and (3) spiritual revival and awakening in my own personal life. Under each of these major headings there could be several subpoints about what you are trusting God for in each of these areas.
- Identify, confess, and repent of all revealed sin before and during your fast. Continue to ask the Holy Spirit to search your heart and reveal any concealed areas where you may feel separated from God. Unconfessed sin and disobedience will hinder your prayer and fasting.

- Be sensitive to the Holy Spirit's prompting in all areas of your life since God will often require you to seek reconciliation or restoration in broken relationships.
- Pray fervently and continually.
- Absorb large quantities of Scripture into your life through hearing, reading, studying, memorizing, and meditating on God's Word. Ask God to reveal what He wants you to read and study in His Word.
- Always reserve time to be still and quiet before the Lord.
- Keep a journal of your purposes for the fast. A limited journal has been provided beginning on page 214. This should contain specific prayer requests, written prayers, devotional thoughts, and spiritual insights you are gaining during your fast. For example, I handwrite many of my prayers to God. I also document whatever I feel God is teaching me, even though they may seem insignificant at the time. I include the specific day and time in the journal entry. These daily writings have been a consistent source of encouragement, strength, and insight long after the fast has ended, reminding me, often months later, of God's direction and calling for my life.
- Skipping meals alone will not result in a meaningful fast! You must *set aside time* to pray and seek spiritual insight. Dedicate at least as much time as you would normally spend in food preparation and eating for prayer and the study of God's Word.

- Consider praying audibly in a kneeling position. At times try getting on your face before God. This may help foster an attitude of humility in prayer and keep you focused on your purposes.
- Praise God verbally and in song for who He is and what He has done. Worship Him.
- Use scriptural prayers during some of your prayer time.
- Ask God with whom, when, and how you may want to share your fasting experience when it has come to an end. If God so allows it, your testimony can challenge, inspire, and help increase the faith of others. Always give God the glory for what He has done in your life.

Physical Suggestions

- As a precautionary measure, check with your doctor before beginning your first fast.
- Eat mainly raw foods and drink plenty of water for a few meals before you begin your fast.
- Decrease the size and frequency of meals before beginning your fast, especially a prolonged fast.
- Determine in advance what kind of fast you will undertake, e.g., total abstinence, water only, water and juice, etc. I recommend water-and-juice fasts. They help you accomplish the spiritual and physical purposes of the fast, while at the same time they help you maintain your energy level and your health.

- Avoid chewing gum during the fast. Chewing activates the digestive processes.
- Days *two through four* of the fast are often the most challenging.
- When drinking juice on a fast, nonsweetened and nonacidic juices seem best. Tomato and orange juice are hard on the stomach, unless greatly diluted.
- Most of my juice was prepared at home. Since I knew I would be entering a prolonged fast, one of the purchases I made was a professional juicer.
- If you (a) undertake a water-only fast, (b) plan an extended fast, (c) have a medical condition, or (d) are taking medication, you should consult a medical doctor familiar with fasting before you begin your fast.
- Consult other resources on fasting.
- You may need to restrict some of your physical activity during the fast, especially rigorous exercise.
- Sudden movements, especially standing up quickly, may cause temporary dizziness or light-headedness.
- Expect some physical, mental, and perhaps even some emotional discomfort. Headaches, sleeplessness, and irritability often accompany a fast, but don't allow the fast to become an excuse for improper actions and attitudes.
- You will likely experience some weight loss during a fast, but the weight usually returns quickly once the fast is broken.

- It's important always to consider the feelings of others, particularly family members, when planning a fast. For example, to plan a fast during a holiday or a family reunion could unnecessarily offend others or draw attention to yourself. Ask God for *the right time* to conduct your fast.

- Some people, even those with good intentions, may try to keep you from fasting; others may encourage you to end your fast before the appointed time. You should anticipate this and be prepared with a kind yet resolved response.

- End the fast, especially an extended one, gradually. After my prolonged fasts, I eat only soft foods for at least a couple of days (baked potato, soup, yogurt, etc.). I begin with small portions and gradually increase my intake. I then move to other foods that are more easily digested. I often wait five or more days before returning to a full meal. Returning to normal eating patterns too quickly after a fast can cause serious medical problems and may also minimize some of the physical benefits of the fast.

ANSWERS TO SOME OF THE MOST COMMONLY ASKED QUESTIONS

Q: How do you know if you're called to a fast?

A: The fasts God has called me to have been as clear and specific as anything He has ever asked me to do in my life. In all cases the deep burden and sincere conviction I experienced were unmistakably from God. Usually, if confusion prevails regarding the fast, it is not God's timing to draw aside. The Lord will make it clear if He wants you to fast, especially for a prolonged period of time.

Q: During your extended fasts, what type and quantities of liquid did you consume?

A: During my extended fasts, the first couple of days I consumed only water. At the conclusion of the second day or at the beginning of the third day, I began drinking various kinds of juices that have been prepared at home in a professional juicer.

My wife would prepare these juices from fresh fruit and vegetables. I most enjoyed juices made from watermelon, cantaloupe, grape, pineapple, and grapefruit. Watermelon juice was particularly effective to reduce an occasional headache. Grapefruit juice helped with the cleansing effect of the fast. Typically, I would drink eight to twelve ounces of juice four times a day. I would consume water throughout the day. On some days I would also drink some Gatorade (because it was refreshing, provided variety, and also helped ease an occasional headache).

Q: What are some of the biggest challenges you have faced during your fasts?

A: Physically, my greatest challenges have come between the second and fourth days. On the first day, because my body was accustomed to caffeine and generous portions of food, the sudden withdrawal caused me to have some major headaches. Later in the fast my body began to feel great. I did not experience any real physical hunger. I had adequate energy and actually felt better than normal, especially after the tenth or fourteenth day.

Although I was not physically hungry after day four or five, I would often face some mental challenges. It can be intimidating and discouraging to focus on how many days remain in your designated fast, especially early in the fast. You've heard the old question, "How do you eat an elephant? One bite at a time." Similarly, "How can you fast for forty days? By fasting one day at a time." It can be a torturous mental battle to count and anticipate that you have twenty or thirty more days to go in your fast. Instead, I remained focused on one day at a time.

Q: How does a fast affect your bodily functions?

A: Fasting cleanses your body. You have to visit the facilities more often than normal. You may experience bad breath or some unusual body odor as the body is freed up to release toxins that have built up in your system.

Q: Have you ever failed in a fast? What should someone do if he or she fails in the fast?

A: No, I've not failed, if failure means not successfully completing the number of days that I had originally committed. I felt deeply that God had called me to the fast, and I remained confident He would enable me to accomplish that which He had asked me to do. If God has called you to a fast and you fail to start or finish, then confess this inaction, repent of it, ask God to give you another opportunity, and then wait for Him to call you to another fast.

Q: What do you write in your spiritual journal?

A: In both prolonged fasts I have recorded many pages of handwritten notes to myself and to God. I will often begin by simply writing, "Dear God," and then continue to write whatever is on my heart. The prayers are usually related to the specific purposes of my fast, but I don't intentionally restrict what or for whom I pray. I also record, "God, You have spoken to me through this Scripture," and then I write down the scriptural reference and the principles He has revealed to me. I always record the date and time when I am writing my journal entry. I also develop a list of things to pray for during the fast. The point is not how many pages you write, but that you record God's working in your life.

Q: What Scriptures do you recommend for study during a fast?

A: Each person should seek God's direction in this matter. Often, when God calls you to fast, He has already given you the passage on which to focus. Isaiah 58 and Luke 4 are good foundations upon which to build your fast. I freely mark in my study Bible, identifying key passages, phrases, or words. I also record notes on its pages. I supplement my Bible study by reading new books.

Q: How do you handle mealtimes with your family or business associates during a fast?

A: During the first few days I draw aside to be alone during mealtime. After a few days I return to sitting with the family at the table. I feel the time of sharing together is important. At that point I am comfortable being around food. The hunger pangs are gone. The food smells good, but I'm not drawn to it. Additionally, each member of my family is aware of the fast and my reasons for it; therefore, they help make the experience pleasant for all of us. I would restrict my lunch appointments, however, and when going out at lunchtime, I simply state, "I'm not eating today, thank you."

Q: How do you know when to plan or schedule a fast (including length and type)?

A: There is no simple answer to this question. I am confident that when God calls you to a fast, He will help you designate the length and type of your fast. Once I was convinced that God had called me to a forty-day fast. I prayerfully considered my calendar and looked for the best opportunity to draw aside for that purpose. The magnitude of the need may determine the length of the fast.

Q: Have you ever been frustrated because God did not answer or lead as a result of a fast?

A: No. One of the results of a fast is increased faith and trust in God and His sovereign will. Of course, I often have unanswered questions, but increasingly I have less and less concern for specific answers to my concerns. I trust God to supply wisdom, guidance, and direction for my every need. True prayer and fasting result in being less concerned about having God confirm or bless my plans, while it increases my concern and awareness for His plans and purposes.

Q: Do you believe women can and should fast in the same manner as men?

A: Absolutely. Although there are physiological differences between men and women, prayer and fasting are not gender specific. Women can and should pray and fast. Several women in our church have gone on prolonged fasts, some for as long as forty days.

Q: How did your family relate to you during the fast?

A: The number one thing my family did was to pray for me. I was encouraged by their prayers, especially during our family prayer time. My two boys, Joshua and Nicholas, were great sources of inspiration to me. In addition, my wife Jeana saw her role as keeping me supplied with fresh juice and water. She faithfully ministered to me at all times.

Q: Did you suffer any adverse effects as a result of fasting? How do you keep from allowing irritability and fatigue from affecting family relations?

A: Although I suffered from a few headaches, I don't believe I had any adverse results from fasting. I didn't have any increased irritability. If I felt tired, I would draw aside and take a brief nap, but this only happened three or four times. My family and I approached the prolonged fasts as something of a journey. They did their best to understand the spiritual significance of the task and were tolerant, even encouraging, of my extra time alone with God and His Word. Although sometimes things around the house were a bit different because Dad was so preoccupied, they all knew this experience would be temporary.

Q: Whom do you tell about your fast, and when do you talk about it? Should I tell anyone about the fast, or is that drawing attention to myself?

A: I believe people who go on a prolonged fast should notify the people around them who will be most affected, which may be only four or five people. I tell these individuals of my intentions before I enter into the fast. My purpose is to help them understand my heart, the reasons for my fast, and to encourage them to pray for me. I am reluctant to share my fast with unbelievers. The teaching of Matthew 6:16–18 on "whenever you fast" is clear on how we should conduct ourselves.

Once the fast is over, I don't believe that telling people about the experience is inappropriate, especially if pure motives are maintained. Think about it this way: Moses received the Ten Commandments while fasting and praying for forty days. Imagine if he had not shared his experience with us. God gave Moses something important in his fast, and he communicated it to the people, including us many generations later. None of the instances of prayer and fasting would appear in the Bible if fasting and its results were meant to be concealed. The key is to maintain a right spirit, a proper attitude, and motives that are pure. Much of what God reveals is a private matter; at the same time you may help expand the faith of others by sharing with them your experience and insights, if God permits.

During the fast do your best not to talk about it unless you are asked and cannot avoid it. Only share about it following the fast and only if God gives you permission.

Q: Do you violate the principles of a God-chosen fast by publicly speaking about it?

A: I don't believe so. Certainly we need to hear and heed the warnings of Jesus issued in the Sermon on the Mount. His instruction does not prohibit all preaching, teaching, and discussion of prayer and fasting; but it does demand that all such communication bring glory and honor to God. If God leads you to talk about your fast with others, do it. Fasting is something God teaches us. Just like praying or any other principle or discipline, as we learn it, we have the privilege of sharing it. As we do, it builds our own faith and helps increase the faith of others.

Q: How should I determine what to pray for?

A: Before I go on a prolonged fast, I ask God for what purposes He wants me to pray and fast. For example, in both of my prolonged fasts, God directed me to pray for revival in America, in our church, and in my own life. Under each of those themes, God gave me ten to nineteen related, specific concerns or topics, e.g., the kind of awakening we need in America and how I would be involved in that revival. I prayed for each of these every day, asking the Spirit of God to teach me what to pray for and what to trust God for during this special time in His presence.

I would begin my prayer time by confessing the sin in my life and then enter into a time of prayer over each of the topics. I would typically end with some other specific concerns. I would then begin my study of God's Word. Usually during a prolonged fast, I would spend up to two hours each morning in prayer, reading the Word of God, and journaling. I am convinced that a person who wants a God-honoring fast will have a similar emphasis on drawing aside to pray and study God's Word.

WHAT TO EXPECT AS A RESULT
OF YOUR FAST

Expect results. A properly motivated and executed fast will have an enormous impact on your life. Invariably the primary place God seems to work is in me. As I am responsive to His lordship and leadership, I find that I must undergo some changes—changes in my thoughts, attitudes, activities, and motives. As I begin to make these changes, everything about my personal ministry and relationships change. Some are uncomfortable, challenging, and difficult. For example, as a result of one fast, I had to confront my pride and arrogance, after which I asked for forgiveness from those whom I had offended. It was important for me to take steps to change the ways I thought, acted, and reacted. Although my tendency for self-worship may resist some of the spiritual principles that God teaches, obedience to God and His Word are nonnegotiable in my life. I am convinced that obedience honors and glorifies God and will conform me to the image of Christ.

God promises to reward and bless true prayer and fasting. I have not found a single promise that God has failed to fulfill. He honors each promise He has ever made. Here are a few of the promises God offers to those who participate in His chosen fast in Isaiah 58:6–14:

- He will set you free from self and your sinful nature. He will loosen the bonds of wickedness and undo the bands of the yoke.
- He will bring freedom from oppression.
- He will transform you into a giver.
- He will give you the desire and ability to meet and minister to people's needs.
- He will allow you to see yourself as you really are.
- God will give you spiritual insight and influence. No matter how dark and dismal the situation, your light will break forth like the dawn. You will help dispel the darkness and its power.
- Recovery and healing of various kinds may occur.
- Righteousness will precede you.
- The glory of God will be your protection and rear guard.

- God will answer your prayers. You will call, and He will answer.
- God will manifest His presence with you. You will cry out, and He will reply, "Here I am."
- He will adjust your attitude. Your gloom will become like midday.
- He will continually guide you.
- He will fulfill your desires in the midst of harsh and adverse circumstances.
- He will give you strength and energy.
- He will make you fruitful like a watered garden.
- He will make you like living water that never runs dry.
- You will become a rebuilder of right traditions and a godly heritage.
- You will become a restorer.
- You will become a repairer of breaches and gaps.
- God will lift you up and exalt you.
- He will give you more faith.

CORPORATE FASTING

Even as I have written about the biblical mandate of personal fasting, one other important issue must be addressed—corporate fasting (the fasting and praying of an entire church or congregation). In the days ahead I will be writing more about this additional opportunity in our churches. In the meantime I pray that pastors and church leaders will come to recognize what "Forty Days of Spiritual Power" can do for the people of God as a whole. This program could be based on every member of the congregation fasting just one day a month, which would mean scores or even hundreds of Christians would be fasting every day for a full forty days.

The purpose of these forty days would be to involve individual Christians in fasting and prayer for the purpose of fulfilling the spiritual goals that churches believe God wants them to achieve. I'm confident that this all-church program could take any congregation to a higher level with God. Why is this program needed? Because individual Christians will seldom go any further than they are led to go in their walk with Christ.

It's my prayer that pastors and church leaders will be persuaded to consider such a program seriously in the days ahead.

SOME CONCLUDING REMARKS

I challenge you boldly and confidently to enter into the fullness of God's will and purpose for your life. True spiritual champions know that when Jesus Christ is not preeminent in their lives they will be open to failure and defeat. True spiritual champions give total allegiance to their Lord. Spiritual champions demonstrate absolute dependence on their Savior and a reckless abandonment to the authority and leadership of their Sovereign. Spiritual champions understand the privilege and responsibility of being children of the King. Human efforts will fail. Natural attempts will not satisfy. Ordinary tactics are finally reduced to mediocrity. There is no lasting contentment apart from God's will and His purpose for our lives. Unless we surrender completely to God's plan, we are destined to drift in a sea of disappointment, disillusionment, and depression. We are in constant need of supernatural power. Our only hope is in the life and love of our wonderful Lord, Jesus Christ.

Revival *will* come. Christians *will* be awakened. The world will be shaken from its catatonic complacency. You can take part and make a difference. "The difference you make *with* your life is contingent on the difference God makes in you. The difference you make in others will never be any greater than the difference which has been made in you by Jesus Christ. The dent we can make in our world will be insignificant without the power of Jesus Christ flowing through our lives."[1]

I encourage you to join with me and many others as we pray and fast for revival and renewal in our own lives, in our families, in our churches, and in our nation.

> Whenever you fast, don't be sad-faced like the hypocrites. For they make their faces unattractive so their fasting is obvious to people. I assure you: They've got their reward! But when you fast, put oil on your head, and wash your face, so that you don't show your fasting to people but to your Father who is in secret. And your Father who sees in secret will reward you. (Matt. 6:16–18)

How to Use This Guide in Your Church for a Corporate Fast

During these seven days, go through this guide at least once. Use this prayer guide throughout the day while you withdraw to be with God. We must get ourselves *in tune* in order to petition and intercede in prayer as God desires.

This guide will lead churches to pray in agreement, especially over the breakthrough we are trusting God to allow in our church. We cannot direct or organize your prayer time for your personal breakthrough. However, please agree with us in prayer over our church's great need for breakthrough, which is specified in this guide. Agreement in prayer is powerful, so let's trust God for a miraculous breakthrough for our churches, ourselves, and one another. Begin the journey to see the walls come down, the miracles occur, and the breakthrough begin!

The guide that follows is an example of the prayer guide that was used at First Baptist Church, Springdale, Arkansas.

My Prayer and Fasting Journal

_____

_____

_____

_____

_____

_____

_____

_____

_____

_____

_____

_____

_____

_____

_____

_____

My Prayer and Fasting Journal

_____

_____

_____

_____

_____

_____

_____

_____

_____

_____

_____

_____

_____

_____

_____

_____

_____

_____

_____

My Prayer and Fasting Journal

_____

_____

_____

_____

_____

_____

_____

_____

_____

_____

_____

_____

_____

_____

_____

_____

Notes

Chapter Three

1. Love Worth Finding Ministries with Adrian Rogers. See http://lwf.org.

2. C. S. Lewis, *The Lion, the Witch, and the Wardrobe* (London: Bles, 1950).

3. J. I. Packer quote; source unknown.

Chapter Four

1. Max Lucado, *A Gentle Thunder* (Dallas, TX: Word Publishing, 1995), 3–4.

Chapter Five

1. Andrew Murray, *Great Evangelical Teaching: Absolute Surrender* (Nashville, TN: Thomas Nelson, 1988), 718.

2. Ibid.

3. Quote from William Booth, founder of The Salvation Army, see http://net.bible.org/illustration.php?topic=317.

4. Ibid.

5. Jim Cymbala, *Fresh Wind, Fresh Fire* (Grand Rapids, MI: Zondervan, 2003).

6. Flora Larsson, *From My Treasure Chest* (The Salvation Army, 1981).

7. "Hymn," *The Magnificant*, February 27, 2009, 371. See http://beautifulcatholicfaith.blogspot.com/2009/02/catholics-believe-in-fasting-during.html.

8. A. W. Tozer, *The Knowledge of the Holy* (Authentic Classics), (Authentic, 2008).

Chapter 6

1. A. W. Tozer quote from *The Expository Files*, "Notorious Noise Noted" by Warren E. Berkley, The Front Page, July 2007. See http://www.bible.ca/ef/topical-notorious-noise-noted.htm.

2. Taken from a James Dobson *Focus on the Family* broadcast, 1996.

3. Martin Lloyd-Jones and J. I. Packer, *Revival* (Wheaton, IL: Crossway Books, 1987), 121-22.

A Practical Guide

1. Ronnie W. Floyd, *The Meaning of a Man* (Nashville, TN: Broadman & Holman Publishers, 1996), II. Used by permission.